OUR BLOOD RUNS BLACK

McClure #1 Mine Explosion
June 21, 1983

MARSHA SUTHERLAND SELF
& REBECCA RINER WHITE

For C's: Christ, Country, Coal, Children

Our Blood Runs Black
McClure #1 Mine Explosion

Marsha Sutherland Self
and Rebecca Riner White
Published May 2025
Heirloom Editions
Imprint of Jan-Carol Publishing, Inc.
All rights reserved
Copyright © 2025 Marsha Sutherland Self
and Rebecca Riner White
Front Cover Photograph of Mike "Buzzy" Sutherland
Cover Photograph by Robin Denise Cochran, Pamela L. Smith
Graphic Design: Tara Sizemore

This book may not be reproduced in whole or part, in any manner whatsoever, without written permission, with the exception of brief quotations within book reviews or articles.

ISBN: 978-1-962561-70-9
Library of Congress Control Number: 2025938440

You may contact the publisher:
Jan-Carol Publishing, Inc.
PO Box 701
Johnson City, TN 37605
publisher@jancarolpublishing.com
www.jancarolpublishing.com

Our Blood Runs Black is dedicated to the hardworking coal miners in the McClure #1 Mine Explosion on June 21, 1983.

Miles Sutherland always carried a little red New Testament in his pocket. It was recovered where the bodies of his co-workers were located. Amid all of the carnage, the Word of God was unscathed and unburned and was laying open to the following verse:

1 Peter 1:7 *"That the trial of your faith, being much more precious than of gold that perisheth, though it be tried with fire, might be found unto praise and honour and glory."*

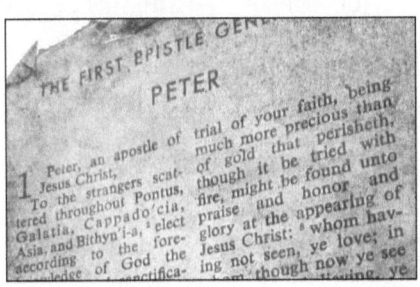

DEDICATED TO THE COAL MINERS
OF SECTION 2 LEFT CREW

Deceased:	Survivors:
Forrest Carter "F.C." Riner, Jr.	Miles W. Sutherland
Luther Mccoy	Emmery Howard
Mary Kathleen "Cat" Counts	Howard Joseph Boyd
Covey French	
Dale Stamper	
Eugene "Houdini" Meade	
Ernest "Ernie" Hall	

Table of Contents

Prologue vii
Marsha Self: Letter to the Reader ix
Rebecca Riner White: Letter to the Reader xi
Rebecca's Poem xii

Chapters

1. Introduction – The Abyss 1
2. Coal Mining Industry 3
3. How it all Began 4
4. Development of McClure #1 Mine 7
5. Ignoring the Warnings 14
6. The Day Shift Crew 16
7. The Explosion – "We Blowed Up, Boys!" 18

8. Section 2 Left Crew – This is Their Stories
    F.C. Riner 32
    Miles Sutherland 41
    "When a Coal Miner Bleeds" Poem 51
    Luther McCoy 52
    Mary "Cat" Counts 64
    Joe Boyd 68
    Emmery Howard 76
    Covey French 79
    Ernest "Ernie" Hall 81
    Eugene "Houdini" Meade 84
    Dale Stamper, Jr. 85

9. "We're Going In" — Darrell Holbrook 103

10. Rescue & Recovery
    Ron Sluss 113
    Norman Lewis 119
    Homer Wayne Fields.. 128
    Danny Mann 140

11. The Wait Outside.. 143
12. Preliminary Report After the Explosion 145
13. The Lure of the Mine 149

14. Co-Workers Remember
    Gregory Austin 153
    Lois Bowman.. 158
    Wade Mullins 160
    Ronnie Mann... 170

15. Conclusion 173
16. Aftermath.. 177

Epilogue 179
About the Authors 182
Thank You 184
Resources 185

Prologue

The room was sterile in its quietness. Moments earlier, it had been a hive of frantic activity. Now, peace had almost settled over the trauma room at the Burn Unit at the University of Virginia Hospital. Miles Sutherland, a 51-year-old coal miner, had survived the worst coal mining accident in Virginia in 25 years. His entire section, Section 2 Left, had been engulfed by a methane gas explosion, killing seven miners and injuring three. He was one of the three wounded in the McClure #1 Mine Explosion and felt blessed to be alive.

Sutherland had suffered third-degree burns over 67 percent of his body, still covered with coal dust and soot from the blast. His work coveralls had melted into his skin. He had just come through the agonizing process of being stabilized...and Code Blue had been called three times.

Burns are often described as the most painful injury one can endure. Only 33 percent of his body remained untouched by the flames.

Sutherland's daughter, Marsha, stood by his bedside, seeking closeness. As she gazed into her father's smoky eyes, she saw him trying to say something. Inhaling the flames had scorched his vocal cords, reducing his voice to a raspy whisper. She leaned in closer to him. He guided her to gaze downward where body fluids no longer contained by his damaged skin had mingled with the coal dust. The mixture dripped and created a dark inky splatter on the floor. In a strained yet proud voice, he said, "See, Angel, even a coal miner's blood runs black."

Letter to the Reader

Marsha Sutherland Self

Upon the death of my parents, I inherited a small blue suitcase that I kept upstairs for a couple of years before going through it. When I opened it, to my surprise, was all the information that my dad, Miles Sutherland, had been given after he returned home from the Burn Unit at the UVA Hospital in Charlottesville.

The suitcase contained newspaper articles from the *Coalfield Progress, Dickenson Star, Roanoke Times, Bristol Hearld Courier, Washington Post, Clinch Valley Times*, personal notes, letters, and the *UMWA Journal*.

At that time, it was 67 days after the explosion. Dad had no idea who had passed or who survived for several weeks after the explosion. He was burned so badly and unconscious, he knew no one.

Dad didn't want to discuss what had happened. He didn't share with anyone what occurred. He just kept saying, "Why me, God? Why didn't you take me? Please take me now. I can't handle the pain. Please take me."

He had survivor's remorse until the date of his death,

almost nine years ago. He had so many great memories of his co-workers and the men that rode to work with him. He loved it. He wanted to go back underground.

The burns consumed all his muscle tissue from his legs and arms. He had to have multiple plastic surgeries for a couple of years. He would always laugh and joke, "When my butt itches, I scratch my face. When my hands itch, I scratch my legs." He was a hoot. I thanked God daily for saving his life. He was never the same after the loss of so many of his comrades in the coal black mine. He loved them and cared for them like family.

This book has been in honor of my dad and brother, Mike Sutherland, who is on the cover, for working so many years in the coal black ground. They kept the lights on for so many of us.

Letter to the Reader

Rebecca Riner White

My dad, F.C. Riner, worked 40 years underground, had three days to retire, and was killed in the McClure #1 Mine Disaster. He had only missed four days of work in a quarter of a century. He was dedicated to the mine and dedicated to his men, had opportunities for advancement but stayed a section foreman, a job he loved wholeheartedly. He loved working in the mine, felt the lure of the mine, and said, "Cut me and I'll bleed coal." It is my hope that our writing honors all miners as we attempt to shed light on a profession that is worthy of recognition. By doing that, we aspire to magnify their contribution to the world.

Even though it has been 42 years since the accident, may we never forget that these men mattered. Their lives mattered, their deaths mattered, their survival mattered. In this book, the intricacies of their daily lives intertwine and weave a work as beautiful as a patchwork quilt. Love lives on.

Long ago in fields of green
My father took my hand,
And led me to the mountain scene
That graced our family's land.

Hand in hand we would go
And walk along the path.
His hand to catch me was never slow
If I stumbled while looking back.

Oh, how good it felt to walk
Through fields of beauty rare,
To take the time to just talk
And feel God's presence there.

I'm sure we quite a picture made
Walking over the land.
Here is where I prayed and prayed
To always have his protecting hand.

But time must do as it always does
And take its toll on all that breathe.
It matters not that it's someone we love.
There comes a time when they must leave.

So now over brown hills and fields
Where the birds sing no song,
Where mountains are darkened with lifeless trees,
A young child walks alone.

But there comes a day when spring will dawn
To awaken all the land,
And the young one who now walks alone
Will take again their father's hand.

— Rebecca Riner White

1

Introduction: The Abyss

Going down, down, down, further into the dark, musky abyss into the core of the Earth. The cage holds 27 coal miners and takes about 25 minutes to reach the dark bottom of the shaft, which is 460 feet underground. It's crowded and warm.

The date is Tuesday, June 21, 1983, the first day of summer, known as the longest day of the calendar year. For some, it would be the worst day of their lives.

There's a lot of joking and talking about what they were going to do for their two-week vacation, which would begin on Friday. Talks included ballgames and vacation plans as the cage descended slowly, deeper into the Earth. There were 84 miners working in the eight-section mine that night. It would change the lives of 10 of them, but 74 other miners would never forget. The deaths bring to 10 the number of miners killed at McClure #1 since its opening in late 1979.

Outside the mine office, a large sign loomed as a reminder of the dangers of coal mining: "June/Vacation Month/Mind on Safety/Do it Safely."

"She's hot. She's got a lot of gas in her," said Junior Felix Boyd.

Once they reached the bottom of the shaft, mantrip jeeps were available to take the miners by rail a mile to the face of the mine, which took another 25 minutes.

Little did they know, not all of them would make the trip back up to see the light of day again. They were the Section 2 Left coal miners involved in the explosion at Clinchfield Coal Company's McClure #1 Mine in McClure, Virginia. This is their story.

2

Coal Mining Industry

McClure #1 Coal Mine is surrounded by the beautiful Appalachian Mountains in the small town of McClure, Virginia, in Dickenson County. The rich coal deposits at the Russell County line are divided by the mighty Clinch River.

The coal mining industry was the lifeblood of the coal camps, providing roofs over families' heads, food on the table, and electricity to the world. Coal was like gold or diamonds — priceless.

Clinchfield Coal Company dominated most of Southwest Virginia and controlled our lives for many years. The land we stood on, and the three-room houses scattered across the entire Appalachian region, were all owned by "The Company." Groceries, clothing, and shoes were purchased — often on credit — at the Company Store in Dante, Virginia.

Even the hospital, where many of us were born, belonged to the Company in Dante. "The Company" owned us, and everything we had was bought with the slips we received from them.

3

How It All Began

In 1898, George LaFayette Carter, a mining industrialist, founded Carter Coal & Iron Company at Crane's Nest on Tom's Creek in Wise County, Virginia. By the end of that year, Carter Coal & Iron Company had acquired land and mineral rights across a significant portion of Southwest Virginia.

Mr. Carter then established Virginia Iron, Coal & Coke (V.I.C.C.), with its headquarters in Bristol, Virginia, in 1900.

The town of Turkey Foot was renamed Dante, Virginia, on January 12, 1903. Carter visited this fledgling coal town on March 9, 1903.

His next business venture stemmed from a dream; to create a railroad that would connect the Atlantic Coast to the Great Lakes via the Coalfields.

That same year, Carter sold mineral rights from his previous businesses to establish Clinchfield Coal Company. The Company purchased large tracts of land in Wise, Dickenson, and Buchanan Counties in the far southwest mountain region of Virginia, absorbing smaller coal companies in the process. Major railroad construction began in 1905.

In the summer of 1906, Carter consolidated all his properties under one company. On June 6, 1906, the newly chartered Clinchfield Coal Company was headquartered in Bristol, Virginia.

By 1908, financial difficulties forced Carter to scale down his plans for the railroad. A new company Carolina, Clinchfield, and Ohio Railway (CC&O), was charted.

Dante was a booming mining town. By 1910, immigrants at Ellis Island were being directed to Russell, Dickenson, and surrounding counties for the coal mining opportunities. Many were directed to Dante. Most were Hungarians, Poles, and Italians. Dante, once called "Turkey Foot," had hollows that connected at the Apex in town and resembled a turkey's foot. Ethnic groups lived in distinct neighborhoods.

The Hungarians, the largest group of immigrants in Dante, lived primarily in Upper Straight Hollow. Greeks lived farther up near the head of Straight Hollow. Another hollow was settled by African Americans. It was called Sawmill Hollow but was formerly known as Seagon Hollow.

In 1912, the offices of Clinchfield Coal Corporation moved to Dante, Virginia.

George L. Carter died in 1936 in Washington, D.C., at the age of 79. He was buried in the family cemetery in Hillsville, Virginia.

During World War II in 1944, the Pittston Company acquired a controlling interest in Clinchfield Coal Company's stock. Subsequently, in 1956, the Company was merged into Pittson Coal. Alpha Metallurgical Resources, formed in 2002, acquired most of the Virginia coal operations of Pittston Company.

4

Development of McClure #1 Mine

In 1979, Clinchfield Coal Company inaugurated McClure #1 Mine, situated off State Road 63 in the Caney Creek section of Dickenson County. Known as the crown jewel of the company, it sliced through a 40-million-ton seam of high-grade coal. As the deepest, largest, and best equipped mine operated by the largest coal producer, it quickly garnered reputation.

Creating McClure #1 Mine was no small feat. Constructing a shaft 460 feet down into the bowels of the Earth. Some mines have a declining slope; McClure's slope was vertical. Imagine going down the length of a 46-story building.

300 coal miners who worked there frequently spoke often of the mine's overriding menace: methane gas! Dubbed a "Hot Mine," it released three million cubic feet of methane into the atmosphere daily, leading to fears of an imminent explosion.

Norman Lewis was employed by Clinchfield Coal Company when the development of McClure Mine #1 began. He describes the initial phase of making the shaft:

"I was on the ground when the equipment arrived. We had a huge hoist that came from Thyssen Manufacturing out of Germany that sunk the shaft, and the slope at McClure was passing mining and German company.

"I mean, it was huge, and we were there and maintenance. So, everybody was outside. In February, we had to get in the bucket, huge bucket that would haul like 10 to 15 tons of coal and go down the center of that shaft, and we would chip off the walls of the shaft because we couldn't work under it. It would be 14 degrees below zero as we were going down the shaft because of all the air that is going down. It was freezing cold. Hanging out of the bucket sometimes 300 feet off the bottom, you could hear the chipping of the ice.

"Now, we're getting ready to start mining. The bottom of the shaft off the concrete, you trim it forward about 20 feet because that's all the space and equipment you have to cut.

"Once the shaft got big enough and far enough in to where we could get a shuttle car down there, the energy started pumping up. We're getting excited! The company opens a nightshift.

"The mining methods we were using was ventilating with rigid fiberglass tubing and the ventilation fans that were on the surface. Every one of us greenlighted the sections we worked on. That was the way of life. The gas was so strong, you could hear it. I mean, it was a constant, like bees buzzing because we learned to respect it. It was new mining.

"We thought the gas was dangerous. We are brothers. Any time you work in that type environment, I don't care who you are…union or not, they are your brother because I'm watching your back. We're watching each other, and that's how it is.

"About six to eight weeks into it, we cut into what would be the intake shaft where the elevator would go. Once we got there, that allowed things to really start picking up. We had a beltline underground.

"We didn't get the huge output that would later come, but that was part of the learning process because everybody that came would have to unlearn what they knew. And many people came that had years and years of mining experience. They would have to unlearn what they had done at other mines to be able to run and operate the mine and keep it safe because of the gas.

"Getting ready to start, they hook that continuous miner to the hoist cable, and it weighed 50 tons. They picked it straight up and dropped it down that shaft 454 feet to the bottom with its rippers frontward and its boom straight up in the air.

"Once they got it on the bottom, they had to have air hoist to pull it forward, because at the bottom of the shaft it was tapered. They didn't go straight down and stop; they tapered up maybe 40 or 50 feet like a 45° angle on all four, set all four directions so that you could bring things in, and later on that became the return shaft, and that's why it was beveled out that way to ease the flow of air. They brought that miner in, got it down there, got a single head Fletcher roof bolter there, and everybody was getting ready to go.

"No scoops. Nothing that would be used on rubber tires to haul the coal out. You would take the miner and cut coal down, load the conveyor, back the continuous miner all the way back into the shaft to the skip bucket, unload it with the conveyor, the miner trims back into the face, and you cut down another load.

"They took the miner, which was a Marietta continuous miner, and it was made for cutting heavy coal for one reason. Clinchfield wanted *that* coal. They had to have something that would cut it better than Eickhoff Mining or Joy Manufacturing, because at that time they weren't making continuous miners that would cut rock and hard coal.

"Here we are! Let's go! Let's start mining! So, came in the next day. And the day shift came out. We had to ride in an emergency elevator called the Dover. It was emergency CAT Dover as a cage and held four people. It traveled at 100 feet per minute. So, it took us right at four minutes to go in and four minutes to come out.

"It took all night long to cut one cut, and it was four to six feet, because in the whole time we're standing there with spotters, that's a methane detector. The machine had methane detectors on it and methane meters, and you could watch the methane go up and down. Everybody on the ground had them. We would stand there turning those things on and off to detect how much methane was actually there. We were that scared of the gas. We really were. We learned to respect it.

"So, shift change at that time was an effort because if you had four trips, you're talking 30 minutes to 45 minutes just getting people down to work. When the first crew came out, I said, 'How'd you do?' They said, 'We got a four-feet cut.' I said, 'We're good.'

"Once the shaft got big enough and far enough in to where we could get a shuttle car down there, the energy started pumping up. We're getting excited! The company opens a nightshift. During that time is when we decided to organize a mine rescue team. It was fascinating because we were not only being trained to preserve and save life; we were training to be in competition with other teams across the nation.

"When you go practice and you'd be under oxygen all day, when you came out, it was unreal. It was like feeling drunk once you started breathing nitrogen again. In the normal air, you actually succumb to a condition called nitrogen narcosis, and it was like two martinis on empty stomach.

"However, miners were leery of the gaseous mine from the outset. We learned that the gas in McClure was different than anything we had ever been around. Once you were in high concentrations, you could actually see the gas. I know it's invisible, it's odorless, and it's tasteless, but when you walked into an area of high gas concentrations, it would look like a mirage on the road. It would actually look like water coming down from the roof when light would shine through.

"You would notice your light shining along the top and you could see that. And you knew before you ever made a check, and you knew before you ever walked into it, that there was a possibility that for some reason there was a lot of gas being liberated."

Despite the region's struggling coal economy, some workers vowed they would leave McClure #1 Mine rather than work there.

Section 2 Left began with three entries. Entry 1, which was dropped on January 23, 1983, reached a depth of 670 feet. The belt and track were located in Entry 2. Entry 3 served as the intake, while Entry 4 functioned as the return. The air used for ventilating the belt and track entry was typically channeled through two-foot vent tubing to the return.

Line brattice and check curtains were employed to direct the ventilating current in the working areas. Line brattice is a partition lining in a coal mine, typically made of wood or heavy cloth. An auxiliary fan, along with vent tubing, was installed in Entry 4 near the #39 Crosscut to manage face ventilation.

The miners enter the mine by means of an automated elevator to the bottom of the shaft. Battery-operated covered mantrips and rail runners are used to reach the working section. Supplies and equipment are lowered into the mine through the slope entry, and supply cars are moved from the slope bottom to the section by battery-powered track locomotives.

Coal is loaded into shuttle cars at the face and hauled to the belt feeder. The conveyor belt transports the coal to the surface.

5

Ignoring the Warnings

Three miners died at McClure #1 between 1981 and the disaster in June of 1983. When the Local Union 2274 Safety Committee Members couldn't get action from management to prevent further deaths, they called for an inspection by UMWA safety experts.

On April 12 of 1983, the UMWA team uncovered 51 violations, including 42 that involved ventilation or fire hazards. The hazards were pointed out to management, and the following day, UMWA Safety Representative Harold Hartsock met with officials of the Mine Safety and Health Administration (MSHA) to express his concern.

Mr. Hartsock said, "I told them that if they didn't clean up the mine and keep it ventilated, they were going to blow it up."

In the nine months prior to the June 21 explosion, federal inspectors wrote 167 violations at the McClure #1 Mine. Only 22 were considered "significant and substantial," or worth more than a $20 fine.

Violations considered not to be serious by MSHA included improper ventilation, inadequate rock dust, accumulation of float dust, and accumulation of combustible materials.

When Monroe West, Safety Director at McClure #1, asked for permission to place battery charging stations in the return airways at the mine, MSHA granted the request two days later.

Other variances requested by Clinchfield Coal Company and approved by MSHA included:

Mining one entry in each section 22-feet wide in order to place the track and the belt side-by-side in the same entry. Using belt fly airlocks in place of permanent stoppings between belt and fresh air entries.

Cutting 22-feet wide where the battery charging stations are placed in order to store two batteries side-by-side.

MSHA's past failure to enforce the law showed dramatically when MSHA inspected the mine July 18-20 in preparation for reopening it.

This time, feeling the pressure from the UMWA and the spotlight of national publicity, MSHA found 186 violations, including 92 that were considered "significant and substantial," more than four times what they found in the previous nine months.

"It was a pleasure to be turned loose for a change," said one Federal Mine Inspector who took part. "For once, I could do my job the way it's supposed to be done."

6

The Day Shift Crew

At 1:30 p.m. on June 21, 1983, the day shift crew cut into fresh air, connecting entry coming from the 1 Left Section. Air from 1 Left rushed across the faces of the 2 Left Section. No steps had been taken to keep the two ventilation systems separate, as required by law. The miners had said that there was more air than usual that night.

Quitting time for the day shift was 4:00 p.m. Long before the horn sounded, coal miners gathered around the elevator, 460 feet below ground. The workers were grappling for position to get on first.

Headlights illuminated the darkness. Clacking along the rails, electric jeeps emerged from the depths of the mine. Lamps bobbing, faces black with coal dust, steel-toed boots crunching in the gravel, another crew ambled their way out.

The last ones on the elevator usually got stuck behind the crowd in the lamphouse where everyone checked in their lamps to be recharged, and then in the bathhouse where miners changed into street clothes. Sometimes, there was a 10-minute wait just to take a shower.

7

The Explosion — "We Blowed Up, Boys!"

The air began to change. It was at the McClure #1 Mine one overcast summer day when tragedy struck.

They all knew that McClure #1 Mine was a very hot and gassy mine, but they had to provide for their families. It was so hot, the ground beneath their feet would boil with bubbles coming up out of the earth.

Most families in Southwest Virginia depended on Clinchfield Coal Company for their livelihood, which included finances, food, housing, clothing, and doctors.

At the time of the explosion in June of '83, Clinchfield Coal Company Management was in a hurry. They needed to have Section 2 Left cleared by vacation time, which was at the end of the week, so they could begin installing the mine's first longwall. President of Pittston Company had stated, "McClure

#1 Mine has the best ventilation system money can buy." But there were serious ventilation problems on Section 2 Left, problems which dated back at least five months to a company decision to drop one of the section's entries.

Section 2 Left began in mid-July of 1982 as a four-entry longwall development section. After nearly six months, it had only advanced 700 feet. Then, Clinchfield management decided to go to a three-entry system in mid-January of 1983.

In the next five months, Section 2 Left advanced an incredible nearly 2,800 feet. Section 2 Left were the best. By June 21, four days before the yearly miner's vacation, the Section was almost done. Remarkable.

The UMWA's Representative, Administrator of Health and Safety, explained why the UMWA opposed the three-entry system: "It just doesn't provide enough intake and return airflow. Four-entry systems are much safer, especially in a gassy mine like McClure #1."

McClure #1 liberates three million cubic feet of methane a day. Methane was a problem in Section 2 Left. The continuous miner had "gassed off" several times, causing delays to reestablish ventilation. When the methane monitor on a continuous miner reads two percent methane, it automatically de-energizes the machine.

Clinchfield Coal Company wanted to use supposedly neutral belt air to help ventilate Section 2 Left, but MSHA denied their request for a variance because the company didn't want to install costly carbon monoxide monitors on the belt.

Jim "Snuffy" Honaker, who worked Section 2 Left on the day shift, said, "But that belt air was getting to the faces most days. When we came in, the curtain at the belt feeder would be down."

Sutherland always felt like he had a guardian angel with him at all times while working underground. His parents were buried above the ground of Camp Branch Mining where he worked for years. He would go deep into the ground underneath the cemetery almost every day for years, knowing he had extra protection overhead. He would say, "I always feel protected with Dad and Mom over top of my head."

God provided this area with an abundance of coal to be used by every continent in the world. It is the world's most abundant energy source. The miners used a lot of dynamite underground to break up rock and coal that couldn't be chipped away with a continuous miner. It was a dangerous occupation.

On the night of June 21, 1983, at approximately 10:15 p.m., McClure #1 Mine, operated by Clinchfield Coal Company, experienced a methane gas explosion. The disaster resulted in the deaths of seven coal miners and injuries to three others. 74 underground coal miners escaped unharmed and reached the surface.

In Section 2 Left, in the middle entry, roof bolters Miles Sutherland and Joe Boyd were beginning their task when the continuous miner, which had just completed a cut of coal, moved to the next entry on the right.

The #40 crosscut of 2 Left had been prepared nine hours earlier. By then, the airflow was insufficient to dilute and carry away the flammable and explosive gases released in the area.

At this point, the crew had shifted to work on the ventilation, and all other work was idled. A beltline used to transport coal was completed. Emmery Howard, Covey French, Mary Kathleen Counts, Dale Stamper, and Eugene Meade were tasked with installing ventilation tubing to prevent buildup of methane.

Ernest Hall, who was Acting Foreman, oversaw their work. French and Howard were on top of the continuous miner, preparing to hang ventilation tubing.

Emmery Howard had been a miner helper for almost three years at the mine and nine years total in the mining industry. His job duties required handling the cable and getting the cable away to keep the buggies from running over it.

Howard recounted, "I would run the continuous miner for the first cut. French would run the miner the second cut. And then we'd take turns." He was willing to take on any tasks, including hanging curtains and placing ventilation tubing. The entire section was focused on ventilation. With some crew members pushing tubing, tightening it, and positioning the slider within five feet of the face.

As the crew worked on Section 2, the belt line was down. Howard took the opportunity to rock dust the area before the coal buggies returned from the top. He placed bags of rock dust on the curtain leading into the middle entry to hold it down, as the air pressure was pushing the curtain toward the far-right entry.

During their dinner break, the buggies returned to the face, and Howard and French resumed their work. French kicked the breaker to turn off the continuous miner while they continued to work on ventilation.

"We didn't hear a boom or anything like that. It was a change in air pressure. Our ears popped and hurt and we felt a big rush of air. It was like a big wind, and then there was a lot of dust," said Jerry Jenkins, who was working in another part of the mine when the accident occurred.

Howard described the explosion: "I was standing on top of the miner with the last piece of wire in my hand to hang it to the last bolt to the face for air. I told Covey I had never seen so much air on this section. We talked, and Covey said, 'Yeah, that's good. That's good. It'll keep the gas out.' We didn't realize the excess air was from an earlier cut and was hampering proper ventilation."

But this night, something was different. It was felt in the air around them. When it was almost dinner time, they rode the mantrip and went over to the "dinner hole" and waited until Riner, who was retiring in three days, made the section.

"That's when it happened. I was turned faced to it. I seen it coming through the curtain; the fire, you know. And after that, I don't know."

He added, "I heard a roaring noise, followed by wind,

smoke, and fire. The fire was coming through the crosscut to me in the face of four entry. When it first hit, the power of the blast knocked my light off my hat and fell to the ground. I couldn't see where I was going or anything. It knocked me back. I don't know how I done it, but I went to crawling, and I could hear somebody going right by me, and it was Covey. He was praying. I could hear him as plain as day. Then I heard the whole area where I was, people screaming and praying, and then, as a matter of fact, in six or eight seconds, it was all over. That was it. It put me out. The heat put me out. It seemed like it was a full force right into us."

Howard collapsed just short of the middle entry. French, however, made it past the checked curtain and turned down the center entry, where he perished. "And then, I guess I was fighting to get out, too. I didn't talk to any of them. I heard Joe holler at Miles and ask him if he was all right, and Miles said, 'Hell, no, I'm burning up.'"

Howard's first recollection after that was Darrell Holbrook, a Foreman from another section, cutting his belt off.

He said, "I didn't know what was going on. I don't know how he brought me back. I was in a bad way. So, he said he was going to check on other men. And when he came back to me, I was as smart as could be. I'd got my senses back. I believe Ronald Neece and a boss from Open Fork helped me out. And they carried Joe, and I walked along with them. They held my arms and brought me out. When we got down to the elevator, they asked me if I could walk, and I said, 'Well, I've walked that far, I guess I can walk the rest of the way out.' No problem. I was in pain, but you can't let that bother you at the time."

Once the men got Howard out the elevator door, he was put on a stretcher and taken to the hospital. It took three hours for the medical staff to clean him up, as he had severe blisters on his face and hands. Lying on his gurney, he saw Sutherland and recalled the shock by the lack of immediate assistance.

"I couldn't understand why they wasn't trying to help him," he said. "If I could have reached my rescuer, I might have saved someone, but the pain was overwhelming. When I reached for my rescuer, my hands went straight back. You're in so much pain and the fire is in your face; you can't do nothing. I was trying to get back to the dinner hole where the big self-rescuer was located. We kept them there or at the transformer. And me, after I got as far as I could go, I knew I couldn't make it that far. They found me between entries 3 and 4 on the corner just before you go through the curtain, I don't know."

Behind French, at the face of the center cut, was Sutherland and Boyd. Boyd remembered nothing of the accident, but Sutherland, like Howard, heard and saw the roaring fire coming down the section toward him.

After the explosion, Sutherland said, "I tried to go down this way here, and Boyd hollered and asked me, 'Are you all right, buddy?' And I said, 'Lord, no.' And then just everything went dark. I got so far, and I went down, and I hollered, 'Help!

Does anybody hear me?' Nobody answered, and that's when I tried to get my self-rescuer off my side. Found my hands were burned so bad, I couldn't get it. And I called upon the Lord, and the last thing I remember saying was, 'Lord, I fully commit myself into your hands.' And I heard somebody say, 'We're coming after you.'"

As death swept through Section 2 Left, bewilderment and the grim realization of a large-scale disaster spread to the other miners scattered throughout the remaining seven units of the mine.

Blake Blackstone, age 43, a Section Foreman that traveled to various mines on various shifts, was working in a far section with a crew of four men when the explosion occurred.

"Our ears started popping, and we just — everybody — commented their ears were popping. We knew something had happened, and dust started coming around us. I took off down the trackway." Blackstone headed to the closest phone. "We got up to 3 Left, and we could smell powdered smoke."

Meanwhile, in another section, Kellis Cecil Barton, a 33-year-old repairman, experienced a more severe reaction: "A big gush of air, rock dust bags, cap wedges, lumps of coal, and everything else came back up the haul way. I was squatted down on my feet beside the jeep, and it pushed me back on my rear end on the bottom; it had so much force to it."

At the same moment, 31-year-old Ronald Chester Sluss, the Assistant Mine Foreman, banged his head as he was coming out of the underground supply house. "The force of the explosion blew the back of the supply house — what we call 'shop mains' — open, and that usually has some pressure against it. And with that commotion, everybody was wondering and talking about what had happened. I never heard nothing except the doors to the supply house open."

By this time, Darrell Holbrook had made his way to Sluss and others. "They thought we had a major roof fall, and I told them, 'No, it was something bad wrong on 2 Left. We needed to get down there and see what we had,'" Holbrook said.

Sluss checked with other sections, which reported air loss. He called the Mine Superintendent, Richard Light, at home and explained the situation. Light made a few phone calls and headed toward the mine.

As other miners began leaving the mine, Kellis Barton decided to take a large jeep and return to his section to retrieve his co-workers, but he met them coming out in a smaller vehicle. "They had all piled up in it," he recalls. "They were on each other's lap, in each other's arms, and everywhere else, which I don't blame them. I would've come out, too."

As others evacuated the mine, Sluss turned to Holbrook and asked, "Will you go with me to Section 2 Left?" They checked self-rescuers and instructed another miner to kill the power in the mine before heading to the site of the explosion. Along the way, they met Blackstone, who joined them.

First, the trio encountered a mantrip, its lights shining toward the outside of the mine. A dinner bucket sat on the mantrip, containing a half-eaten sandwich, two peaches, and a set of false teeth.

"Of course, I seen how hot it was and how the jeep was scorched," Sluss recalled. "I thought at that time it had blown up from the section. I didn't realize that was the mantrip jeep that Riner and McCoy apparently had been riding. It was black and hot. I know you couldn't have laid your hand on it and rested it there."

As they continued, they discovered a boot that was not burned and had no shoelaces. They discarded it, thinking that it was unrelated to the accident. They had to turn back. They needed fresh air, and they began to zigzag through the mine, taking gas readings as they moved forward. Their readings varied between two-tenths and three-tenths of a percent of methane.

Holbrook coughed a few times. "I asked him if he was all right," Sluss remembers, "because I knew he had some mine rescue training, and I knew he'd get dizzy if he got in the carbon monoxide. I asked him on two or three occasions if he felt all right because I knew I did. But I didn't know if someone else would feel it first. Because I was scared."

There was dust near Section 2 Left. "There may have been smoke. I wasn't realizing it was smoke, but I remember my mouth was very dry. I could not even hardly spit."

As the miners walked up the middle entry, Sluss heard Sutherland. "I heard Miles holler, Miles Sutherland. I knew Miles. I knew his voice. I knew it instantly. It was Miles hollering."

Then, they discovered Covey French. Holbrook checked his pulse. "Nothing." Sluss and Blackstone then found Sutherland standing with his hands on the roof bolter.

"He knew he had been in an explosion," Sluss commented. "Sutherland hollered, 'We blowed up, boys.' I told him, 'Yeah.' And then he prayed, and I prayed with him, trying to keep him settled down."

One by one, others were discovered: Boyd, unconscious; Howard, babbling out of his head; Stamper, no pulse; and Eugene Meade, who apparently survived the initial blast, kneeling, his head down, but no pulse.

The men decided to move Sutherland first. Holbrook remained underground with the injured men. Sutherland was praying. "And he would say, 'We're not going to make it, are we, boys?' Over and over, he'd say that to me," Blackstone said, choking up, then regaining his composure as he detailed the scene.

"And I would try to tell him, you know, everything was going to be all right. Sutherland tried to jump out of the jeep on many occasions; he was burned so badly."

When they reached the outside with Sutherland, volunteers were ready to return inside with them. They had accounted for seven of the ten miners that were supposedly on Section 2 Left.

When the rescuers returned to Section 2 Left to search for the remaining miners, they discovered more hard hats than they had found people. "We knew something was wrong," Kellis Barton remembered. "So, we went to digging; you could see a light shining up out of the dust." It was the light of Mary Kathleen Counts, the first woman to die in a Virginia coal mine explosion.

Barton relates, "I felt under her throat to see if she was alive. I told Blackstone I believed I felt a heartbeat, but mine was beating so rapid, you feel for yourself."

But Blackstone found nothing. Barton urged him to try again. He had to rake the dust off her arm to feel her pulse in her arm, and he said, "No, there is no hope." There was no hope for Riner and McCoy, who were later found by the mine rescue team 2,400 feet away, down the first entry and beyond the mantrip.

Miles Sutherland and Joe Boyd were at the roof bolting machine facing Entry 3 when the explosion occurred. Their CH_4 registered 0.7 and 0.9 percent, respectively. With his experience as a Fire Boss, Sutherland felt comfortable proceeding with such low readings. However, the explosion's force pushed him back, while Boyd has no recollection of the events.

After finding Boyd on the mine floor with no detectable pulse, the rescuers made a crucial third check. Miraculously, he had a pulse with shallow breathing! He remained unconscious and had no memory of the explosion.

As three mine rescue teams arrived, they were informed of the three surviving miners in Section 2 Left. The rescue crew entered the mine while Ron Sluss, Blake Blackstone, and others worked to bring Sutherland to the surface. At 11:45 p.m., Sutherland was loaded into an ambulance and was transported to a hospital in Wise, Virginia.

Sutherland suffered third-degree burns over 67 percent of his body. A small, red New Testament that Sutherland carried in his pocket every night was found near his lost crew members, opened to 1 Peter 1:7.

"That the trial of your faith, being much more precious than of gold that perisheth, though it be tried with fire, might be found unto praise and honour and glory at the appearing of Jesus Christ."

8

SECTION 2 LEFT

Section 2 Left was well known as having had the most experience and was also known to have yielded the highest coal production. An excellent leader was F.C. Riner, with 40 years of experience. Ernie Hall was taking the foreman position since Riner was retiring at the end of the week.

There were 10 coal miners on Section 2 Left the night of June 21, 1983: F.C. Riner, Miles Sutherland, Luther McCoy, Mary Kathleen "Cat" Counts, Joseph Boyd, Emmery Howard, Covey French, Ernest "Ernie" Hall, Eugene "Houdini" Meade, and Dale Stamper, Jr.

Forrest Carter "F.C." Riner

His Story

Forrest Carter Riner, Jr., went by the moniker "F.C." Others simply called him "Riner." He was born in the small town of Clinchco, Virginia, in Dickenson County, on July 20, 1924, to Forrest Carter Riner, Sr., and Carrie Belle Campbell.

His family made their home on Sandy Ridge, Nora. Descending from a generation of coal miners, he was a slender, wiry man with a memorable laugh and a twinkle in his dark eyes. He loved family, farming, gospel music, and coal mining.

His love for coal mining was challenged by his love for sunshine, but he had to make a living to feed his nine living kids. He went to work in the mines when he was just 17 years old in 1941. He took to coal mining like a duck to water and had worked his way up to Foreman in 1967.

He worked at various coal mines over the years; among them were Lower Banner Coal Company, Pocahontas, Red Ash, and Big Rock, to name a few. With the mines, in 1956, he went to

Clinchfield's Moss #2 Mine and was a shuttle car driver and was transferred on May 28, 1982, to McClure #1 Mine.

He had been a Union man for 17 years, and becoming a "Company Man" would take some adjustments, but he was thankful for the increase in pay.

Forrest Carter "F.C." Riner, Jr.

Yes, he loved coal mining and the sunshine. Very sad that one was at odds with the other. When he came home from a long day at work, he would ask, "Did the sun shine today?" He didn't know, because he was in the mine all day. He occasionally quoted the great poets, but his favorite was Emerson: "Be still, sad heart, and cease repining; behind the clouds is the sun still shining." He loved Emerson's "Rainy Day" poem, and he loved the coal mines.

He enjoyed listening to gospel music and had an amazing singing voice. After going to school with Carter and Ralph Stanley, he learned to harmonize singing in church and in the school yard. His mother and the Stanleys' mother went to church together on Dog Branch, not far from where the McClure Mine would be one day. He frolicked and played in fields not knowing their connection to his future. Underneath lurked the mine where he would meet his fate.

When he was little, he wandered the mountain acres that his family owned. He collected rocks and looked for "Indian" graves, marked the way his father taught him. He and his father would walk paths made long ago by elders and ancestors whom he was taught to always respect. His father talked of years past, when the chestnut trees were towering, as big around as a car. Sadly, an Asian blight settled over them in the early 1900s, and they became extinct.

In the evening, sunset came early to the ridge as the sun went behind the enormous mountains, and he disliked the early dimness. His mother told him, calling him by her pet name for him, "Little Brown, never be afraid of the shadows the mountains cast. That is your forefathers watching over you." Riner loved the mountains.

At 22, F.C. met his future wife, Edra. She was two years older than him. F.C. made up his mind to marry her, and he altered his age to do it. Not wanting to be younger than his bride, he came up with a bogus birth certificate. They were married June 28, 1944, and shared a union and 11 children (two died in infancy) together until the day the disaster happened.

Riner's retirement was originally planned for May 24, 1983. While compiling all his information, it was discovered he had two birth certificates with different birth dates. He was asked to work 30 more days so this could be straightened out and validated. He agreed. His retirement date was changed to June 24, 1983. The McClure Mine disaster happened on June 21, 1983. He was killed three days before his retirement date. Changing that birth certificate altered his destiny.

He worked a hard life: homesteading, farming, and coal mining. He and his family worked 15 acres of land, living in a home with no running water. It's been told he had a joke about the water: "I do have running water. I tell Ed (Edra) to run and get the water, and she brings it back home. My Indian name for her is 'Running Water.'"

Tragedy struck when they lost two baby boys within two years of each other. One died of crib death, and one never made it home from the hospital. The baby died three days after birth due to a congenital heart condition. Two times, F.C. Riner held dying infant sons in his arms and could do nothing to stop the Angel of Death.

He clung to the faith of his youth, using gospel songs as his prayers: "Pass me not, oh, Gentle Savior, hear my humble cry. While on others thou art calling, do not pass me by." (A Stanley Brothers tune.)

Yes, hard work, family, gospel music, and the coal mines defined him. The family had their fair share of tragedy over the years, but the boys were helping work the land and going to school, and the girls helped their mom around the house and made stellar grades. He still had his "Running Water" by his side, and now he had "little running waters" that helped with the chores. The older children were graduating.

Near year's end came Christmas. Anticipation and excitement were always in the air in the Riner household during this time. The fall had been productive, the harvest plentiful; fruits and vegetables had been canned and were on the shelves. Furniture graced the living room that Ervinton High School had given the family. It was looking like one of the best holidays yet, until tragedy struck.

On Christmas Eve, December 24, 1965, a pair of work coveralls hanging over the coal stove caught fire in the basement. The fire spread through the house like lightning. There was no water to fight the fire, but Edra and the kids did their best against the flames. The roaring fire consumed everything. When F.C. drove down the dirt path to his mountain home, it was burned to the ground. Nothing was saved.

His kids came running to meet him, faces smeared with black soot, and eyebrows singed. Edra, with a baby in her arms, was in the distance looking like she had fought a war. Thankful everyone survived, but his heart sank as he realized he had nothing left.

Neighbors who helped the family standing along the path saw something no one had ever seen before. F.C. bowed his head onto the steering wheel of his vehicle and wept.

Friends helped the family any way they could. In return for working the land, a vacant farmhouse was found for the family to live in. By 1967, Riner was made Foreman and things began to look up. He worked in a shaft mine, Moss #2, and drove many miles from the mountain to get there. In 1971, he and his family moved to the coal mining town of Dante, Virginia. It was closer to his work, and they had a home with indoor plumbing

Yes, Riner loved his job, often racing his pickup truck to work and arriving early. Records indicate he had only missed four days of work in the last quarter century. He took more safety readings than required for a boss and did not like when his men questioned his authority.

In 40 years underground, he had earned and demanded respect. It often frustrated the company that he asked for more rock dust than was allotted. Some called him "The Preacher of the Rock Dust."

On June 21, 1983, it began unusually for Riner. Delays crept into his day as he was preparing for his 4 o'clock evening shift. One, in particular, was a flat tire on the pickup truck he drove to work every day. While driving into the nearby town of St. Paul, he had a flat at Hanging Rock about three miles away. Luckily, a neighbor happened along to help Riner.

As the afternoon progressed on, he said, "Riner, don't go into work today. We're having so much trouble getting that tire, you're going to be too late to make your shift."

Riner said, "This is my last week of work. I'm outside this week and don't have to go underground. The new Foreman, Ernie Hall, is taking over this week."

Even though he didn't have to go underground, Riner had planned to eat with his men. He had even planned a chicken dinner for his last day that week. He and the neighbor got the tire changed, and he made it to work on time. A flat tire almost saved F.C. Riner's life.

That same day around 5:00 p.m., as Riner was manning the desk in the office, a call came in for supplies to work on a problem with the drive chain on the feeder on Section 2 Left. Riner saw this as an opportunity to go help out and have dinner with the men.

He got a ride in the supply buggy and arrived at the section around 7:00 p.m. By 8:00 p.m., repairs were completed and he enjoyed dinner with the men.

Riner understood the hazards of his job but was particularly concerned about the dangers of McClure #1 Mine. He had said, "It would surely become a graveyard when it blows."

In 1958, at Moss #2, he had survived an explosion on his shift that killed two men. He had lost two brothers-in-law to accidents. He was quoted as saying, if there ever was another explosion on his section, he didn't want to live if it took his men.

Survivors remember Riner being excited as he talked about bringing them dinner on his last night. One co-worker stated, "F.C. Riner thought the world of his men, and they thought the world of him." Over the years, there were many opportunities of advancement for Riner, but he chose to remain a Section Foreman because of the rapport with the workers.

Father's Day fell on Sunday, June 19, before that fateful Tuesday in 1983. Riner's family members have fond memories of that precious day. With his children and grandchildren gathered around him, Riner regaled them with talk of his upcoming work week. He was to be "VIP" for the week; no duties would be assigned to him, and he would be above ground in the office until his last day, Friday, June 24.

He had a chicken dinner planned with all the fixings to take down to the dinner hole to eat with his men on his last day. Which, as a surprise, was to be Thursday night, not Friday. He wasn't going in that Friday because the miners had a hazing planned for his last day — to cut his pant legs off, among other job-related pranks. He told his family that Thursday would be his last night, and he would eat a special dinner with his men.

"My last meal will be with my men," he said emphatically. Little did anyone know, but Riner's *last* meal would be with his men on Tuesday night, not Thursday.

Forrest Carter "F.C." Riner, Jr.

Rescue found Riner's dinner bucket on a buggy and saw that the inside contents were undisturbed by the blast. There was a half-eaten bologna sandwich and two whole peaches.

Riner will live on through his children throughout eternity: Dwaine, Connie, Dudley, Sue, Dean, Randy, James, Louie, Eddie, Lily, and Becky. They have many memories to cherish — his love for Christmas, the treats he always brought home in his dinner bucket, running to meet him as he came home from the mine, him sitting outside under a shade tree singing, working in the garden, and his love for animals. He instilled in his children the gentle admonition to "be somebody." He would tell them, "Anything worth doing is worth doing right."

Riner was a man of faith. He loved his family more than anything and died providing for them. He will forever be the diamond shining in his family's hearts.

Front: Dwaine, Edra (wife and mother), and Eddie
Back: Randy, Duck, and Dean

Front: Lily and Edra
Back: Connie, Sue, and Becky

Miles Sutherland

His Story

Miles Sutherland provided a detailed account of his activities at the time of the explosion. "I was pinning in the Entry 2, and we didn't have trouble with gas the whole shift."

However, a major ventilation interruption occurred, affecting the airflow in the two sections and leaving approximately 3,000 feet of Entries #1 and 2 in Section 2 Left without positive means of ventilation in virgin territory. This area, a longwall panel with a history of high methane liberation, was left in dangerous conditions.

Sutherland had previously expressed his concerns to his family, particularly about his son, Mike Sutherland. He feared the mine would eventually blow, though he didn't know when. His anxiety about leaving his wife, Mary, and his daughter, Marsha, without his support weighed heavily on him. He always tried to protect and provide for his family.

He accepted his Lord and Savior Jesus Christ in 1972. This

faith gave him the confidence and strength to continue working amid the dangers of the mine.

At home, safe in his living room, Sutherland often stared straight ahead, shaking his head in disbelief. He was consumed by the thoughts of the mine. "Why? Why not me?" he would ask, grappling with the reality of his life intertwined with coal mining. The smell of coal was as unforgettable to him as the most expensive perfume might be to someone else.

After midnight, he would pull out his Johnny Cash albums and play them on his massive stereo cabinet, which he was immensely proud of. Although he couldn't carry a tune, by the second or third drink, he felt like the Man in Black himself. He would flat foot until he couldn't anymore.

Sutherland worked hard to provide for his family and enjoy the small pleasures of life. Christmas in the coal camp of Trammel, Virginia, was a special time. O.T. Austin, who owned a small store and gas station at the edge of town, would receive the presents from Miles and Mary. O.T., also running a wrecker business, played Santa Claus exceptionally well. After midnight on Christmas Eve, the sight of his wrecker truck with its red flashing light through the darkness seemed to signal the arrival of Rudolph and Santa. O.T. enjoyed the cookies but seemed to prefer something stronger to keep him warm while delivering presents.

The memories of those Christmases are precious to Sutherland. He recalls the joy of watching O.T. play Santa and the excitement of the coal camp. Friends would come over on weekends to blast dynamite at the old tipple behind their house, shaking the entire camp.

The explosions would rattle the neighborhood, and all the families would listen from their back porches, laughing at the antics of Miles Sutherland, Joe Shortt, Bill Baily, Ed Kiser, and others. They even broke several of their neighbor Margie Shortt's whatnots out of her windows, even though she never discovered who was the guilty party.

Miles Sutherland had been a coal miner most of his entire life. That's all he knew from a young age; born and raised on a remote mountain top of the Appalachians in Dickenson County, Virginia, called Hazel Mountain. He was the 15th child born to Pastor Thomas W. Sutherland and Carrie Tennessee Hicks. Coal was already in his blood, and the lure of the coal mine was all around him growing up as a child. It was pulsating underneath his feet and deep inside the very mountain that he called home.

With nothing but an eighth-grade education, the coal mine called his name, and he went underground for the first time at the young, tender age of 13. Miles served his country in the 101st Airborne Division of the Army. After serving his country, which he loved, he returned to underground coal mining.

Miles Sutherland in the Army

"They say it turns your blood to black, and I believe it. When you came out, you were black from head to toe. You could scrub and scrub and never wash it all off. It seeped into every crevice of your body. It was hard, dark, damp labor, pulling coal out with donkeys in the beginning; with a shovel in one hand and a canary in the other to make sure the air wasn't toxic with gas, we would work 10 or 12-hour shifts.

"The strangest thing about working underground is you never know when it is daylight or dark. It's always dark. It is the darkest night that you can imagine. So dark, you can't see your hand before your face. We carried small lanterns to find our way into the mine and had lights on our hats while we were working and pulling and chipping away at the coal in the middle of a mountain. But this night, something was different. You could feel it in the air around you."

It was almost dinner time, so Sutherland rode the mantrip and went over to the dinner hole, and he waited at the dinner hole until the Foreman made the section. After eating an egg sandwich, a Little Debbie oatmeal cake, and putting a piece of peppermint gum in his mouth, he put his dinner bucket down and headed to the face of the roof bolting machine to bolt the roof.

"I was a roof bolter at that time," he said. "Me and my buddy, Joe. There was no problem on the Section, so we started bolting roofs in the middle entry, which we call Number 2. I could feel the air. It was coming from the left at the setup entries and into my face. That was the only entry I had been in, unless I was in another one that night, and I don't remember. This was a special night for some of us. Our Foreman was retiring, and the miners two-week vacation was at the end of the week. We all looked forward to miner's vacation and seeing daylight for two weeks straight every day.

"I always ate with the men for about 10 minutes, and then I would read my little red New Testament that my daughter had won repeating scripture. So, I had my fried egg sandwich and oatmeal cake and headed to a place where I prayed usually every evening for the night to be safe and for us all to go up that shaft together, but I couldn't that night. I didn't have no glasses with me. I couldn't see to read it. As I was leaving the dinner hole, the Foreman started walking with me, and I said, 'Old man, what are you doing in here anyway? Why don't you stay outside?'

"And Riner said, 'I'm going outside right away. Luther McCoy is going to take me outside.' That was the last time I got to see and speak to Riner. Me and Joe just kept on bolting in the face of the mine."

At 1:30 p.m. on June 21, 1983, the day shift crew cut into fresh air connecting entry coming from the 1 Left Section. Air from 1 Left rushed across the faces of the 2 Left Section.

"It seemed like there was more air than usual that night," said Sutherland. "I was pinning in the No. 2 Entry, and we didn't have trouble with gas the whole shift. But while the ventilation system problem at the 2 Left faces seemed to be resolved, mixing the air on the two sections caused a major interruption in ventilation. This change in the 2 Left's ventilation left approximately 3,000 feet of Number 1 and Number 2 entries of Section Left with no positive means of ventilation in virgin territory along a longwall panel with a history of high methane liberation."

Contained in the entries with no positive means of ventilation were the section's power center, the belt, the track, energized trailing cables, and other electrical equipment, all sources of a potentially lethal spark that was in the making and was inevitable. Methane built up for nearly nine hours. Somewhere, there was a spark. At 10:15 p.m., the spark ignited the methane, and the resulting explosion ripped through Section 2 Left, killing seven and injuring three.

Miles W. Sutherland was a survivor of the explosion at McClure #1 Mine that fateful night. When the accident occurred, he was 51 years old. He planned on retiring as a coal miner in the years to come. The explosion ended his 27-year career as a UMWA coal miner. When Camp Branch Mine closed in June of 1982, he was transferred to McClure #1 Mine and started his first day on November 29, 1982.

Having 14 siblings wasn't easy when it came to dinnertime. Sutherland's dad always told Miles, "If you don't make it on time to dinner, you don't eat."

The 15 children would fight and trade for food. With one last biscuit waiting on the plate for someone to get, Sutherland went for it, but his sister Gertrude was faster and stuck her fork in his arm and took the biscuit with the other. He still had the scars from the prongs imbedded into his arm when he died. Little did he know at that time, as a hungry child fighting over a biscuit, years later over 67 percent of his body would be burned. However, the scar remained untouched and visible in his right arm until the day he died.

Sutherland's life changed on June 21, 1983. "It seemed like there was more air than usual that night. I was pinning in the Number 2 entry, and we didn't have trouble with gas the whole shift."

But unknown at the time, the air on the two sections caused a major interruption in the ventilation system. This changed in 2 Left's ventilation and left approximately 3,000 feet of #1 and #2 entries with no positive means of ventilation in virgin territory along a longwall panel with a history of high methane liberation.

After 67 days in the UVA Burn Unit, Sutherland stated, "Clinchfield was in a hurry up there. They were always pushin'. They wanted to get that section done before vacation so they could put that new longwall in."

His voice was just a whisper because of the severe, permanent, damage to his vocal cords from inhaling the flames from the explosion. "I was pinning in the Number 2 face when I heard a noise. It sounded like a high-pressure hose had blown apart. When I turned around, I saw a wall of fire and smoke coming at us so fast you wouldn't believe it. It was like a fast freight train roaring towards us. All I had time to do was cover my eyes, and I remember saying, 'We've blowed up, boys.' I don't remember much more except for the pain was beyond anything I could ever imagine. We've got to do something to stop them. We can't let this kind of thing happen ever again."

Sutherland's daughter, Marsha, stated in the UMWA Mining Journal, "It was June 22, 1983, at 12:50 a.m. when I answered the telephone. It was Wise Hospital telling me that my father had been in a mine explosion at the McClure #1 Mine. Only a few people could possibly know how I felt at that instant. The nurse told me that he was alive and was being transferred to Holston Valley Hospital in Kingsport, Tennessee. The hardest thing I ever had to do was to tell my mother.

"The hospital was an hour drive, which seemed like an eternity. The doctors were already working on my father when we arrived. They advised us that we could see him only for a minute and to show no emotion. I was so nervous walking into his room. He said, 'Hello, Angel,' and I shattered inside.

"The once handsome man that I knew as my dad was no longer before me. His hair was burnt orange, and his skin was black and shiny like an onyx stone. The doctor informed us that there was nothing they could do and would be transporting him by plane to the University of Virginia Burn Center in Charlottesville, Virginia. The nurse came into the hall and gave my mother an envelope and said, 'He wanted you to have this.' It was his gold wedding band. It was no longer a round, eternal circle. It was straight as an arrow after having been cut off his finger.

"Only the pilot, a nurse, and a doctor could go on the plane.

We all had to drive the five and a half hours to Charlottesville. The most devastating part of the ride was that we heard on the radio that Dad had not made it and died in flight. We were emotionally distraught. We agreed to continue to the hospital where dad was being taken to. There was no turning back. Our prayers were that he was still alive and the news was incorrect.

"We arrived at the hospital at 11:00 a.m. He was alive. The doctors advised us that he had third-degree burns over 67 percent of his body. From that day on, it was operation after operation, graft after graft. On July 1, he awoke enough to realize what had happened. He prayed for his buddies that had lost their lives and for God to give strength to their families.

"The family was by his side for 67 days that summer to help him get through what most of us will not endure in a lifetime, but we knew that it was God watching over my father that night. His Bible was found by the superintendent, and it was opened to 1 Peter, 1:7: '*That the trial of your faith, being much more precious than of gold that perisheth, though it be tried with fire, might be found unto praise and honour and glory at the appearing of Jesus Christ.*'

"My dad and my brother, Mike Sutherland, worked their entire career underground as coal miners. They loved it. Additionally, I worked at the United Mine Workers' District 28 Office in Castlewood, Virginia, for eight years. We all knew what it meant to be a part of the union. This is a time that we all need to stand together and fight to get us where we are today. Together we will stand and never be defeated."

Miles Sutherland, one of UMWA's finest workers, had more than 27 years in and worked his entire life underground.

Miles and Mary Sutherland

Miles Sutherland

The Sutherland family
Front: Mike and Mary (wife and mother)
Back: Miles and Marsha

When a Coal Miner Bleeds

There once was a story...a legend by now,
'Bout some men that worked by the sweat of their brow.

Many may question if this story is true,
But it happened to more than one of the crew.

It occurred one day as coal miners mined,
On an ordinary day, in an ordinary time.

Gas had built up, the very air was methane,
And when the mine blew, the blast was insane.

It took 7 lives, but 3 survived...
A miracle that not all miners died.

The whole section bled, all were taken aback,
'Cause the miners' blood turned black!

Those who saw it that day were never the same;
Saw it's coal that flows in a coal miners' veins!

So the stories are true, and now you can know,
When a coal miner bleeds, he's bleeding out coal.

— Rebecca Riner White

Luther McCoy

His Story

Luther McCoy was 36 years of age and had worked as a coal miner for 16 years, and although he had never had a close call, he was certainly aware of the hazards of the job. McCoy started working at McClure #1 Mine on January 7, 1983. He was a member of McCoy's Chapel Church serving as Sunday School Superintendent. He was a member of the United Mine Workers of America.

Nola Mullins, the widow of miner Luther Julian McCoy, still gets choked up when thinking about her deceased husband. McCoy married young and had their first daughter by the time they celebrated their second anniversary.

McCoy wanted his wife to have an education so that if the need ever arose, she could provide for herself and their daughters. McCoy had worked in the Moss No. 2 Mine for 15 years, but when it closed down, he took a job at McClure #1. He knew the mine had a reputation for being gaseous.

But he had a family to support and needed the job. Besides, McCoy was a conscientious man, having previously received 10-year and 15-year pins for safety. Nola graduated from college in May 1983. Within a month, her beloved husband would be killed.

McCoy worked the evening shift and usually returned home from work around midnight. His wife, who always waited up for him to return home, remembered that it was after 1:00 a.m., and well past time for him to be home, when the phone rang. No one ever wants to receive that call.

A neighbor said that there had been an explosion at the time and asked if McCoy was home. Mullins immediately called her brother-in-law, Darrell McCoy, who picked her up and drove her to the mine site.

Nora recollects, "We were stopped by security. When they found out my husband was in the explosion, they allowed us to go on up. We were taken in a secure area with other family members. Not knowing much of anything, we all prayed that somehow the men may have found an area and be safely awaiting rescue. Within a few hours, family members learned the miners had been found and were deceased. We were not allowed to see them, as their bodies were badly burned and recognizable only from the tags each miner wears just for this kind of identification."

The families and community were shaken and grief stricken. McCoy's daughters, Veita and Anna, were 16 and 12 years old. They both loved their dad so very much. At first, there was denial, then came acceptance and grief.

McCoy said that her daughters were hardened toward the mining company, believing officials had allowed safety to be ignored, which cost them their dad's life. They were comforted only by their memories of him.

"They were old enough to keep him in their hearts, keep the lessons he taught, the morals he instilled, and the love of God in their hearts and souls. The hardest thing we have experienced is not being able to tell him goodbye."

McCoy worked in the mines the majority of the 19 and a half years they were married. "Spouses learn to accept the coal miners' choice to work underground. The miners have a brotherhood, much like the police, firemen, and others. Safety is always a concern, and the brotherhood of coal miners — a family, one might say — will watch out for each other. Miners don't dwell on the fact that when they go into the mine, they may never again see their families," Nola said.

Nola believes they often keep hazards and uneasiness hidden from the spouses so they won't worry. "Yet danger is always prevalent and on their minds. Curtains could have been in place; more rock dust could have been thrown. A spark ignited the methane and disaster was the result. Was safety ignored or simply forgotten?"

She still ponders that question years after her husband was killed in the explosion. "The 'what-ifs' will be forever in my mind." The death of her husband left a void in Nola's life that will forever be with her, yet she states, "Life goes on."

"Remember, there are folks at home waiting for your shift to be over." Her prayers continue with all coal miners and their spouses. "I pray that miners who continue to make a living in the coal mines and their wives have found solace and comfort with the savior."

The loss of her husband was felt not only by his family, but his church family and community as well. "His death continues to be a loss to all who knew him," she said. "We will never forget him or the other six whose lives were lost on June 21, 1983."

The family made their home in the Brushy Ridge section of Dickenson County. They were active in their church, where they both taught Sunday School. It was her ability to work so well with children that spawned Mullins' desire to become an elementary school teacher, an idea her husband whole-heartedly supported.

Vieta Lyle

Survivor of Luther McCoy

"My dad, Luther McCoy, was killed in the explosion at the McClure #1 Mine on June 21, 1983. He had been wanting to quit the mine for a long time. From what I understand, his father, also named Luther McCoy, had died in a coal mining accident at the same age — 36. Dad's accident had a similar outcome. He was caught in a rock fall that struck his head, causing a blood clot. He went to the hospital, but unfortunately, he died after several days.

"Dad married my mother, Nola Skeens, when she was just 16 and he was 17. They lived on Brushy Ridge. From what I've heard, they started dating before she turned 16, and her mother didn't like it at all that she was dating a McCoy boy. Mom dropped out of school, and my dad had a plan. They moved to Illinois where Dad worked in a box factory. I was born there, and at the age of three, we moved back to Southwest Virginia because Dad wanted to work in the mines, like many people from our area who went to Aurora, Illinois, to work in factories.

After 14 years in Illinois, the McCoys returned to Southwest Virginia. "Dad loved working on cars and was a mechanic at heart. There wasn't a car he couldn't fix, and when he wasn't in the mine, he was always under the hood of a car. He dreamed of opening a little garage on Brushy Ridge to work on cars, but he didn't get that chance. Mom decided to go back to school. She earned her GED and then went to Clinch Valley College, determined to become a schoolteacher. She graduated in 1983, and it was her plan that once she got a teaching job, Dad could finally quit the mines and pursue his dream of working with cars."

Vieta recalls, "This is the God thing. Mom graduated in May, and Dad died in June — just when he was about to quit the mine, right after Mom got a teaching job. Dad had worked so hard to get us to this point, and he wanted out of the mines. He knew his father had died there, and Mom didn't want him to work in the mines anymore either.

"In May 1983, Mom graduated, and in August, she got a teaching job at Ervinton Elementary. But tragically, Dad didn't live to see it. I'll always remember him talking about how proud he was of Mom and how he was going to quit the mines once she started teaching. But God had other plans.

"I graduated from Ervinton High School, and my younger sister, Anna, also graduated. We were just starting to build our future when we lost Dad. We had always been a close family, and we were active in church. I remember getting baptized in the creek at the bottom of the mountain, and our family always went to church on Sundays. But after the explosion, everything changed.

"I often wondered why some people survived and others didn't. I always thought the explosion had killed everyone. There were only seven survivors, and I still question why my dad didn't make it. There were 84 miners underground, and my dad was in one of the sections hit hardest by the blast. But somehow, he survived the initial blast. He was at the face of the mine with Joe, another miner. They were close, but Dad made it out. Joe didn't.

"The explosion was caused by a buildup of gas. Dad had always said the air was thick with it before the explosion, and they knew something was going to happen, but they didn't know when. My dad was getting ready to leave when the blast occurred.

"Afterward, I questioned everything—why didn't my dad survive? Why were some miners saved, while others weren't? There were so many unknowns about that explosion. The mine should have been shut down before it happened. The supervisor was in charge, and the gas levels had already been high. Yet, they allowed the miners to work.

"I've had a lot of time to think about it. The devastation of losing my father so suddenly was overwhelming, but I know that life goes on. My mom raised us with strength. Despite her grief, she became a teacher and supported our family. We carry on the legacy of our loved ones, even when we don't understand why they were taken so soon.

"My dad's story is part of me, and it's woven into the fabric of who I am. He was a man of hard work and determination, and I will always carry his memory with me, even if the world forgets. The impact of his loss still affects me, but I've learned to live with it. It's just something you have to accept, but you never stop missing them.

"That night, before Dad left for the mine, he came to me and kissed me and Anna, as he always did. I didn't get to say goodbye in the way I wanted, but that was the last time I saw him. I hold onto those moments now, and I'll never forget the love and care he showed us, even in the toughest times. I miss him every day.

"After the explosion that killed my father, I lived with my mom and family, trying to process everything. I remember feeling a mix of shock, disbelief, and deep sorrow. I had always been close to my dad, and his loss hit me harder than I could have ever imagined. Mom, however, remained incredibly strong through it all, even when it felt like everything around us was falling apart.

"I remember one particular night before the explosion, I had a conversation with my mom about my dad. We were talking about how strict he was and how he didn't approve of my dating. As a teenager, I didn't always understand his rules, and in my rebellious mind, I sometimes resented him for it. But I also knew he loved me and wanted the best for me. That night, I remember thinking how frustrating it was to be so strict, but I never expected that night to be the last time I saw him.

"I was at home when the phone call came in. It was late, around 1:00 a.m. I had been out, but my sister and I were both home when my uncle Darrell, Dad's brother, arrived with terrible news. He had come to tell us that there had been an explosion at the mine. My mom screamed and cried, and I felt paralyzed. My uncle took my mom to the mine while my sister and I stayed with him at his house, which was less than a mile from our home. We didn't know the extent of the situation, but we feared the worst.

"Mom had always been the strong one, waiting up for Dad every night. I had memories of her staying up late, always worried when he was working. Dad worked in the mines, and we knew the risks, but we never expected it to happen to him. After the explosion, I remember my mom's reaction — complete devastation. She was strong for us, but I could see how much it hurt her. She had to hold it together for me and my sister, but I know the pain she carried in silence.

"The loss tore not only our immediate family apart but also affected our extended family, including my mom's side. My uncle Tommy quit working in the coal mines after Dad's death. He couldn't go back. And while some of the family handled it better, the weight of that day stayed with all of us.

"The days following the explosion were a blur. I remember being in shock, not able to fully process what had happened. I didn't cry at my dad's funeral. Instead, I sat there in disbelief, thinking that somehow, he would walk through the door any minute. I was just too stunned to grieve properly. People came to our house with food, trying to comfort us, but it all felt so surreal.

"In the days that followed, my family struggled to keep it together. Mom had always been the glue that held us, but I could see the toll it took on her. She had to take care of everything, from dealing with the funeral arrangements to supporting us as we tried to navigate life without Dad. I'll always admire her for the strength she showed, even when she was breaking inside.

"I remember feeling ashamed sometimes, especially when I was younger, because we were a Pentecostal family and didn't always fit in with the more conventional community around us. I was embarrassed when we had to use food stamps or when my dad's strictness felt suffocating. But looking back now, I realize how much my parents loved us and how hard they worked to provide for us. They sacrificed so much, and I didn't understand it all at the time.

"After the explosion, everything changed. The world I had known, with my dad working in the mines and my mom always being there for us, was gone. The day he died, I remember feeling completely lost. I didn't know how to move forward. But one thing I knew for sure was that my family would continue to survive, just like my mom did. She may have been shattered, but she found a way to keep going — for us.

"The pain of losing my dad hasn't gone away, but I've learned to live with it. What I've come to understand is that even in the hardest times, there is hope. My family's faith has helped us through, and while life will never be the same, we have each other. And that's something my dad would have wanted for us.

I'll carry his memory forever, and though I never got to say goodbye the way I wanted, I know he loved me. That's the one thing I will always hold onto.

"I remember we had a basement in our house, but I can't recall the door leading to the basement. For years, this has haunted me. I would wake up in the middle of the night, hearing banging on the door, and I'd think it was my dad. He used to work on cars in that basement, and I wondered if he had just lost his memory, not really dead but out there somewhere, trying to find his way home. For years, I had dreams where I opened that door, and it was him — alive but with amnesia, trying to come back.

"I never saw his casket. I think that's why I couldn't accept his death. Not having that closure messed with my mind. When I look back now, I realize how important it is to see someone's body to understand they're gone. But I never had that. Many people don't have open caskets anymore, but back then, it was the norm. I never got that chance.

"I still have a cassette tape of my sister and me singing with him. It's the only thing I have left of his voice. I've kept it all these years, but I don't have a cassette player anymore. My dad never spoke much about his past, and we never really had deep conversations. He'd tell stories sometimes, like the time he ran around with his brothers in the mountains or carried guns. I cherish those stories, but I never knew much about his life.

"Joe, my friend, recorded hours of conversations with his dad before he passed. He learned so much about his father through that, even discovering his real birthday by accident. It made me realize how little I knew about my own dad.

"When I was young, I was always fascinated by family stories. I've tried to capture some of my own life in writing, thinking about the future. I've written 50 chapters, mostly for my kids. My family wasn't as open with their history as I would have liked. There was so much trauma and hardship that I didn't understand until much later.

"After my dad died, things shifted. People assumed we were well off because of workers' comp, but we didn't get much. I married young, and my mom worked hard to make ends meet. It wasn't the glamorous picture people imagined. My dad's injury was devastating. I didn't know how to process it all, and honestly, I don't know if it would have been better to see him like that or to have remembered him the way he was before. But my memories of him are mostly from before the accident, and I never had the chance to see him afterward.

"In the end, I found out more about my dad's life from his journal and letters. I wish I'd known more while he was here. The story of his injury and the years after are all scattered, but I'm piecing it together. It's not much, but it's something.

"As I reflect on everything, I realize how much I've missed. I never had the full picture of my dad's life, and now it's too late. But I hold onto the memories I do have and the stories that were told to me."

Mary Kathleen "Cat" Counts

Her Story

Being known as Virginia's first woman to die in the coal mines, Mary Kathleen "Cat" Counts lived her life through her children. She raised three girls and two boys after her husband died in an oil well accident in the 1960s. She was born on January 24, 1932.

She was an exceptionally beautiful young woman who grew into a very attractive woman. Some said that in her heyday, she looked like Marilyn Monroe.

Cat Counts outlived two husbands, divorced a third, and reared five children before she became one of Southwest Virginia's first female coal miners. It was a job she loved — a job that satisfied her.

She had a tender toughness about her — toughness that earned Ms. Counts respect in a profession dominated by men, tenderness that led her to nurse dozens of stray animals. Her daughter, Bobbi Rasnick, shared with us that her mom had

32 animals that she loved and nurtured. Cat became known as the "Unofficial Non-Human Aid Society."

Cat faithfully attended a small country church, the Church of the People, where she was one of the founders.

Before working in the mines, she worked at the local Dickenson County food co-op. After leaving there in 1978, Cat went to work in the mines to provide a better life for her children. Cat enjoyed success in her role. During her life, she worked at three different coal mines, including Open Fork, Splashdam, and finally, at the McClure #1 Mine.

Mary Kathleen "Cat" Counts

Cat's great sense of humor and playful banter helped her soften the hardened miners. She had been laid off 17 months before being hired at McClure #1 Mine in March of 1981.

She started out shoveling coal onto the conveyor belt that climbs a sloped shaft from the mine to the surface. Because of her perseverance in shoveling coal, she earned the nickname "Continuous Miner." She had recently completed training to operate a shuttle car, which carries freshly mined coal to the conveyor. She was driving one the day she died.

A native of Nora, Virginia, she was the fifth woman to die

Cat Counts

underground and the first woman casualty in Virginia. She did what she thought was right, regardless of what anyone said. She had a tender spot in her heart.

She was one of a kind, capable of giving it out as strongly as the miners gave it to her. She had a sense of humor and gained the respect of her coal mining co-workers.

After enjoying her favorite drink, Dr. Pepper, she hung the cans along the track of the mine. Other miners always kidded her about it. "Why do you do that, Cat?" they would ask. She always answered, "Because when this baby blows, I can find my way out."

On many occasions, she fed the rats while she was eating at the dinner hole. Another question would always arise: "Why in the hell do you feed those nasty rats?" She replied, "Because if they turn and run the other way, I'm going with them. They're smarter than we are."

At her funeral, the pastor said, "In the spirit of Jesus and the prophets who challenged the rich and the powerful...I think we do need to ask the question, 'When is the coal industry going to get right with God?' Some serious questions need to be raised about an industry that could, without mercy, gobble up land and mineral rights 60, 70, or 100 years ago, literally paying pennies for what has meant millions of dollars for a few, while severely exploiting its workers and resisting, without mercy, their attempts to organize unions for better working conditions at the mines. Questions need to be raised about an industry that, throughout its history, has seemed to have lost its soul in the pursuit of gaining the whole world."

Howard Joseph Boyd

His Story

The week of June 20 was going to be a big one in Joe Boyd's life. On Friday, miners' vacation would begin, and on Saturday, Joe was to be married to the love of his life, Renee. The McClure #1 Mine disaster changed his wedding plans.

"I was lucky." He married Carolyn Renee two weeks after the explosion. "I got out with only a concussion and a few burns. I can't remember anything from that whole week after the explosion. I didn't know how I would feel when I went back into the mine."

Trying to think back, Boyd states, "We had a good crew. We worked with each other, and we depended on each other. Our biggest problem in Section 2 Left was getting methane detectors that worked right."

After the accident, Boyd had a severe redness to his face and permanent memory loss that still affects him to this day. He writes notes down, and his wife helps him remember people, places, and times. Across the middle of his forehead is a form of indention that is a constant reminder of the disaster. As the mining hat came off, the impact of the blast blew him into the top of the mine, hitting his head.

Boyd stated after the explosion, "I'm glad I made it out somehow. But there's seven who didn't. I wish they could have made it, too. I can tell you what I can remember. I stayed down at my fiancée Renee's Sunday night."

Carolyn Renee and Joe on their wedding day.

"I was in my early twenties, but there were some even younger than me that got killed. And, of course, there's some a lot older than me that got killed. When it happened, the rescuers went by me and checked my pulse three times, and the third time they found a very faint pulse and brought me out."

All that Boyd can recall is stopping at the car wash in Bristol, Virginia to wash his old Jeep on Monday. He does slightly remember getting out of the hospital on Saturday, and the rest of it is totally blank. Boyd has sought treatment for his memory loss in several different medical facilities. He only found one physician that made sense.

Joe and Carolyn Boyd

"I went back to work. I officially retired about 1988. Somewhere in that area. I don't have no short-term memory. I forgot about this interview. My wife reminded me of it and posted a note on the bathroom mirror and in the kitchen. I carry a pencil and a piece of paper in my back pocket.

"And you had a number on your belt that had your name and social security number on at all times. That is beneficial to know that everybody is accounted for. When it blowed up, they had your tag because you had to tag out. When you go in, you have tag on. It looks like dog tag when you're in the Service. It is about that same length and that same width. And it was solid brass and wouldn't burn. That possibly could be the only form of identification for a coal miner after an incident. But now, that was the strange part. They found my belt, even with my name on it, but it had not been burned.

"During my time underground, I wore a face shield because I wore prescription eyeglasses. Miles didn't wear one. He didn't need glasses. I wore my name on safety glasses. They looked like regular glasses. Then they introduced new safety shields where you drilled a couple of holes in the hat. There's a little piece of metal that you adhere to the shield so it can be flipped up and down.

"Once, we needed supplies from the surface. They would load them onto the elevator and send them down. Supplies were unloaded and placed into a stock room. People would come and inspect the cables, pulleys, and everything on the elevator for certification. When you got off the elevator, get on a mantrip jeep to go to your section. It took Miles and me about 45 minutes to get to the roof bolter at the face of the mine to begin work. Maybe 30 minutes.

"Now, the track that goes up to the supplier is operated by a switch. The main entrance to the mine is called a slope, and it's something like 1,700 feet on a fault, almost 45 degrees. At one time, while they were unloading a new continuous miner, they let it break loose from the top. It had broke apart. The miner was high up on the flat core and half out. When they broke it, the miner was going down the shaft, so we jumped out of its way, and it went airborne halfway down the slope. Now, we're talking about 140 tons.

"It not only destroyed the new continuous miner coming in; it destroyed everything it went into. I'm talking about 10 toilets, water lines overhead at the bottom of the slope. I think we were shut down for a week and a half trying to replace all of that equipment.

"I went to work at McClure #1 Mine the first part of 1982, January '82, because that's when I met Renee, and I went to work right after I met her. I met her on New Year's night or New Year's Eve, and then I went to work in January there in 1982, and then I worked the whole time up to 1983.

"I was off work for six months before I went back to work. I looked a little sunburned. But no, nothing like my buddies. I just looked like I'd been out in the sun for a day with rain. It didn't ruin my green coveralls.

"The crease crawls all the way across my forehead. That's now a thin line I can feel. It sent me into the roof for a moment. The force was so violent. My hard hat was busted. My hat had a little sticker holding it together on that side and my head on the inside. It had clips on. That's what was holding it together. Well, I don't know what it done to my memory.

"The night of the accident, Miles said, 'I feel a difference in here,' right before it happened. It boils down to where you were at up on the section. There was one place on the section that should have had a block wall, but a curtain had been placed there instead. There was a hole cut through into the section coming across. That's where I was at.

"So, we were getting plenty higher up in the face. We were making progress getting higher up on the face. I would say this was uphill all the way. We had to be careful always because of rocks falling. Some guy had died with Miles earlier that year. I can't remember his name. It was a rib roll that killed him. Had a rock come out of the side of the mountain and it killed him.

"Now, the Riner man, the boss going to retire at the end of the week, he was in the mantrip. McCoy was taking Riner back up to the surface. Both of them were killed. Blowed them out of their boots, they said. They said it was the pressure of what happened at that instant can do that.

"Well, I didn't get to none of the funerals because I didn't get out of the hospital in time. I had a bunch of security around me when I got out of the hospital, and experts trying to tell me what to say. Like, 'Well, this brattice was broke down this way and the other brattice broke down the other way, and this brattice was blown down this way,' and it kept going.

"They were telling me the reason that the brattices were blown up toward the mantrip jeep is because the explosion blew the doors open and let the pressure out. We just had three working sections because we had started out with four when we dropped that one out. So, you had one, two, three.

"The reason Miles got burnt so badly is because it didn't knock him out. He kept standing. The fireball came straight down the section on his side of the roof bolter. You don't see what it is. What the expert told me is when it blows in one area, you feel the pressure first. It's like a bullet being shot out of a gun. You get the pressure first. The pressure comes around and then it stops. It goes around so far and stops and then comes back around the second time. Brattices blowed out one way as the explosion passed, and when the fire turned around and came back, blowed the brattices in the other direction. That relieves some pressure.

"Holbrook, Sluss, and Blackstone did not wait for a mine rescue. They walked past me two times and thought I was dead. They could not get a pulse. On the third time, they took my pulse again and they finally got a pulse.

"After the mine explosion, I went back to work in the McClure #1 Mine. I was asked, 'How can you go back in there and work after what happened?' I told them, 'Well, I mean, in memoriam.' It was just like I had a long vacation and went back to work. The trouble is, I couldn't get rid of headaches and couldn't figure out why. I played football for years and got hit in the head on many occasions, but I never had a headache.

"I was told that Ernie wasn't burned because he fell face forward into water. Some of them had crawled around before they died. I'm talking about when they found some of them, they were over in a different area and so forth. I could tell that they were there. The report said they were all looking for air. Miles, I think, was looking for air when he must have stumbled across some of them when he had his Bible out. He lived it. He saw it. The Bible was found in a different place than where he was located back at the face.

"I remember waking up in the hospital, and there wasn't

nobody in the room, but I could tell I was in the hospital. I remember looking around and having hand bandages on me. And I said, 'What the heck am I doing in the hospital? You might as well tell me what happened.' They started telling me, and I didn't remember any of it. I didn't want them telling me what I didn't want to hear. The Lord stayed with me all the time.

"Riner didn't have to come underground that night. He wanted to visit. It was McCoy taking Riner around on the Main. McCoy was the mechanic on Section 2 Left. McCoy was taking Riner out on a mantrip jeep when it blowed up.

"I always loved working in the mines."

Emmery Allen Howard

His Story

Howard was a devoted family man with four children who loved to sit on his lap. At the time of the explosion, he was married to Susan Helen Woods and shared four children — Crystal Woods, David Allen Howard, Joni Howard, and Stephanie Howard.

He and other workers had raised concerns with the company about dangerous conditions that led to the deaths of five UMWA members — Covey French, Eugene Meade, Mary Kathleen "Cat" Counts, Dale Stamper, Jr., and Luther McCoy — and two supervisors, F.C. Riner and Ernest "Ernie" Hall.

Although company officials were slow to protect miners on the job, they were quick to act whenever miners insisted on safety. Howard recalls, "I told them I wanted to check the gas first myself. The foreman told me to either take the miner up there right now or get my bucket and get on the jeep because he was taking me out. So, they took me out.

"There was always a lot of gas up there. We asked for more air and more rock dust, but it was like the company didn't even hear us. Our whole 2 Left crew went before work a couple of times to the Mine Superintendent and let him know. We were worried about the gas and the air. The supervisor wouldn't talk to us."

Emmery Allen Howard

Howard was on the continuous miner with French when it exploded. "It ripped my light cord in two. I was stunned, but I started crawling in what I thought was the right direction. Then it came again; I don't know if it was another explosion or just the first one going around again. Sometime between the first blast and when they got me outside, I heard almost everyone on that section. I could pick out each individual voice. They were all crying and praying."

They had all informed the Company about the hazards that led to the tragedy, but their requests for more air and rock dust fell on deaf ears. Nothing was changed. "The McClure #1 Mine had the best ventilation system money can buy," they were told, yet serious ventilation problems had plagued Section 2 Left for months, stemming from a company decision to reduce one of the section's entries.

He remembers what happened when he and Meade, who was killed in the explosion, had told their boss several months earlier that they wanted proper checks for methane gas. "The boss said to tram the miner to the face, that there was only .7 percent methane there, but we checked, and it was 2.7 percent. So, we worked to get the gas out. We tightened curtains and such. Then the boss told us he checked it again, and it was okay and to run the miner up there. So, I told him I wanted to check the gas first myself. He told me to either take the miner up there right now, or get my bucket and get on the jeep, because he was taking me out. So, they took me out.

"Later that night, the foreman called me, regretting his decision to fire me. The next day, Local Union 2274 officers and committee members met with the superintendent, who acknowledged the firing had been a mistake."

David Allen Howard, his son, shared that his dad always loved working with all of them. He always said that they were his family. At its very core, Section 2 Left were family. They lived by the coal miner's bond: one of brotherhood, unity, and selflessness.

Covey French

His Story

"French believed in three things," his wife, Murrell, said after her husband was killed on the night of the explosion. "His family, the Holy Bible, and the Union." He was survived at the time by four sons, Mikey, Danny Allen, Covey Jack, and Clinton Ray, and two daughters, Brenda Lee Rose and Peggy Louise French. He was a member of the Hill Ridge Freewill Baptist Church. He had worked at McClure #1 since June 21, 1979.

Murrell always prayed and was concerned about her husband as he would leave for work. "He was worried," she said. "Lately, he'd been talking about how the mine was unsafe. He kept saying the gas was getting real bad. Then he went to work that day, and he never came back."

When the rescue team found Eugene, he was in the kneeling position with his hands together.

At his funeral, Covey French was remembered as a "child

of God" who "left a testimony behind." At the service, a fellow miner from McClure #1 shook his head and quietly remarked, "Covey was one of the safest miner operators I know."

Ernest "Ernie" Hall

His Story

Ernest "Ernie" Hall had worked for several different locations for Clinchfield Coal Company during his career and had just returned to McClure #1 Mine. After speaking with his lovely wife, Debbie McInturff, Ernie, at age 30, was returning to become the foreman of the evening shift.

Having worked there for a short period of time in 1981, he always talked about it being a hot mine. He and Debbie knew the dangers.

Ernie was a quiet, loving man, slightly built with long black hair and a moustache. He was known to be a good man and nice person, with a smile always on his face.

He was a member of the Castlewood Lions Club. People liked him, but he didn't make a forceful impression. He didn't have to. Everyone he met liked him. The men referred to him as "the young boss" to distinguish him from the previous section foreman who remained on the job for his final week of work.

He was very close to his parents. He had two older brothers, Ken and Rufus. All three brothers worked in the coal mining industry. His sister Diane was the youngest. His brother Ken worked the hoot owl shift at McClure #1 Mine. "Hoot owl" is the shift that begins at 12:00 a.m. and ends at 8:00 a.m.

Ernie loved working on cars, especially an older model Camaro. He built his own motorcycle in his parents' basement. He was named after a bagboy that worked at Dante Company Store. That is how he got his middle name, Avery.

Ernie and Debbie were married at the Assembly of God Church in St. Paul, Virginia, in 1975. Their beautiful daughter, Brooke, was born on August 20, 1977. He loved spending time and playing games with her. He would turn her upside down, "walking on the ceiling."

On that horrible night, her aunt and uncle pulled into the driveway, shining their headlights as they came up the road. Debbie knew it wasn't Ernie; knew it was about Ernie and the mine. She could tell Uncle Rufus was crying, and she yelled, "Stop, don't tell me!"

In the early morning hours, the house became full of people. Brooke didn't understand what was happening. Debbie took her to the bedroom and said, "Brooke, God needed your daddy to come and be with Him." Brooke said, "Don't He know we need him more?" Brooke didn't go to the graveside. Ernie had one little bruise on his forehead. He was placed in a mausoleum. He had always told Debbie,

"If I die underground, please don't bury me underground." It was an emotional graveside service.

Brooke recently said, "Coal miners are like police officers. You never know what a shift will bring."

Ernest "Ernie" Hall

Brooke Hall (daughter) and
Jacqueline Averie (granddaughter)

Eugene "Houdini" Meade

His Story

Eugene Meade, known as "Houdini" because he often seemed to vanish, had been a miner for many years and a member of Local Union 2274. He was married and had children. His wife's name of the time was Sharon Gibson Meade. They had one son, Travis Eugene Meade. Houdini had four brothers and one sister.

His buddies called him "Houdini" because they couldn't find him most of the time. He always disappeared.

He started at McClure #1 Mine on August 17, 1981.

Standing at his brother's grave, James Meade remarked, "The company always claimed they had the proper amount of air. But if there is still gas, then, in my opinion, there's not enough air. Eugene went to work in the mines before me, even though I'm older. He took me under his wing and showed me the ropes. Now he's dead. His death was unnecessary. It should never have happened."

Dale Stamper, Jr.

His Story

Dale Stamper, Jr., was a quiet family man, married to Ella Jean Taylor. They had one son, J.D. Stamper, and three daughters, Carol Salyer, Beverly Boyd, and Teresa Edwards. He was a Christian of Baptist faith.

He was a proud veteran of World War II and a member of the United Mine Workers of America, Local Number 2274, and had worked in the mines for the past 17 years.

Russell County, Virginia, was his lifelong residence in the Carterton Community. His dad was a railroad man, and his great grandmother was a full-blooded Cherokee Indian.

At the time of the explosion, he was classified as a utility man and had worked in that capacity for 13 years and had a total of 17 years of mining experience.

In December 1982, Stamper completed and received his Annual Refresher Training, which included Hazard Recognition.

Dale Stamper, Jr.

Dale and Ella Jean

He really enjoyed a game of horseshoes with his co-workers at the mine property before heading underground. Watching the NASCAR Winston Cup Series was his favorite pastime, and he loved baseball.

The Ghosts of 2 Left Crew

It was some years back, and long ago, when the mine blew...

But folks still talk, and the stories flow about the Ghosts of 2 Left Crew.

Curtain is still down, boys, whatcha gonna do?

"Leave it," said the bossman. "Leave it for the 2 Left Crew."

Ain't no worry for the Big Man...2 Left Crew's mistakes are few.

They'll hang that missing curtain; they'll know that gas is high.

With 2 Left Crew on the scene, not one man will die.

But Section 2 Left Crew was down by one on that fateful day.

And once a spark lit the air, there was little time to pray.

But they had been the safest shift, careful so long.

So, when the mountain finally blew, she only took her own.

No one could hardly believe it...so many still alive!

But the families of 2 Left Crew could only pray and cry.

And so, from Chile to West Virginia, where mine fatalities are few,

Now, you know how the story goes...They were saved by the Ghosts of the 2 Left Crew.

— Rebecca Riner White

Marcus Johnson

Marcus Johnson, currently employed as a coal miner, pictured with Aubrey, Jeremiah, and Gabriel.

View of continuous mining machine located at the face of the No. 4 entry.

View of roof bolting machine located at the face of the No. 3 entry.

Fly curtain located in the No. 40 crosscut between the Nos. 3 and 4 entries.

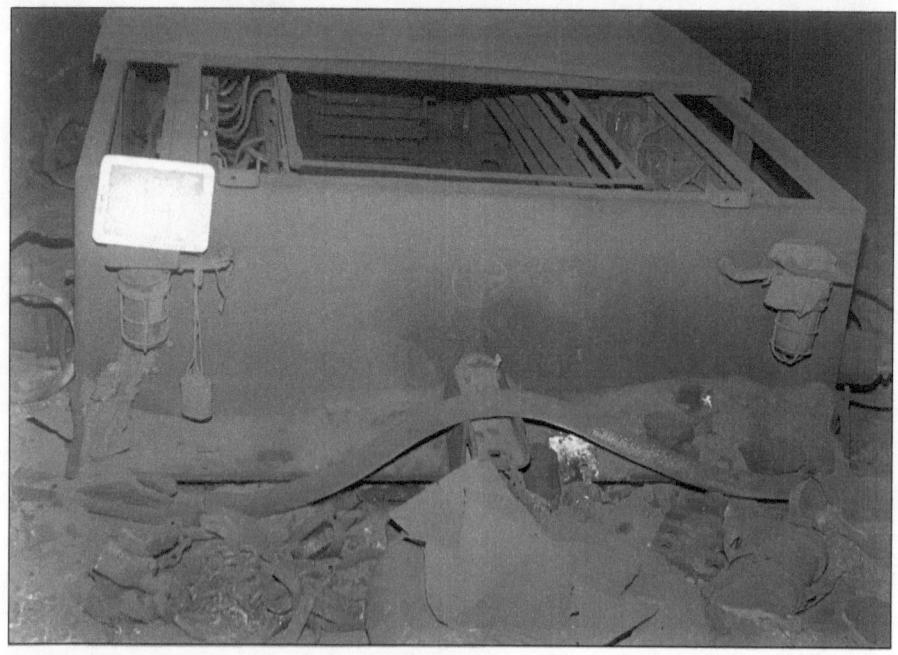

View of the inby end of power center.

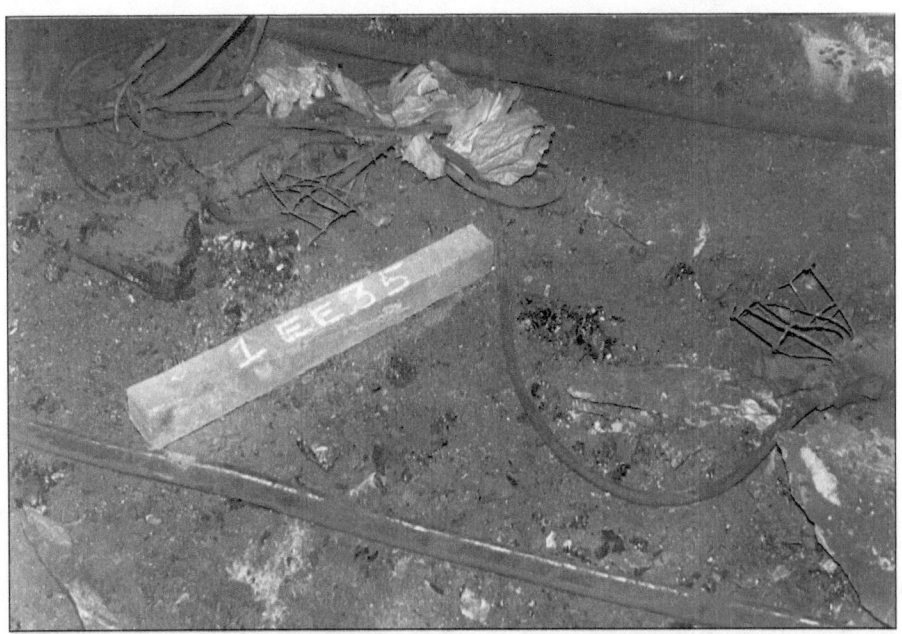

Portion of the power center lightning circuit and supply cable marked "Dinner Hole Lights" found 150 feet inby the power center.

Inby end of the 2 Left section personnel carrier.

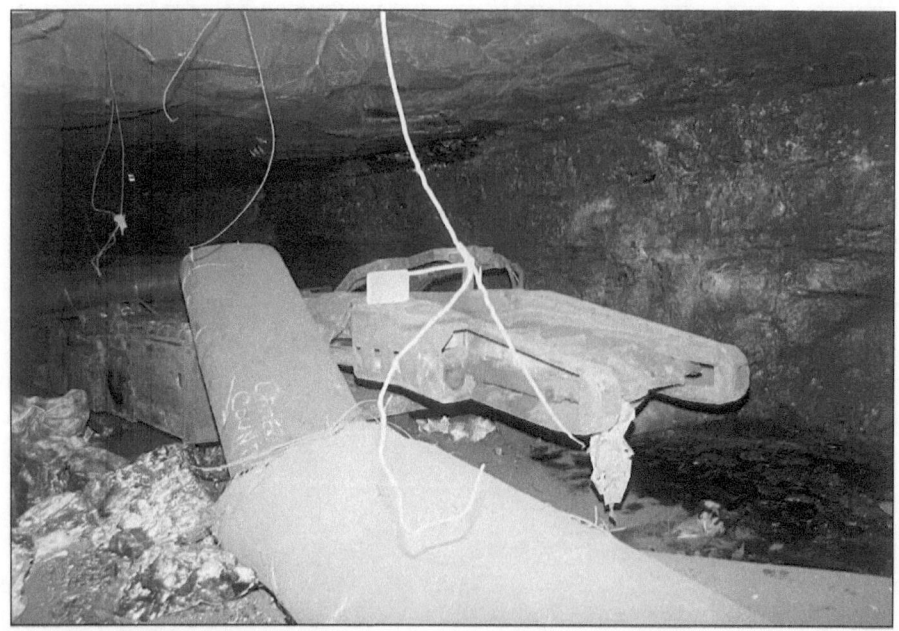

2 Left – continuous miner

2 Left – continuous miner

2 Left – ventilation tube

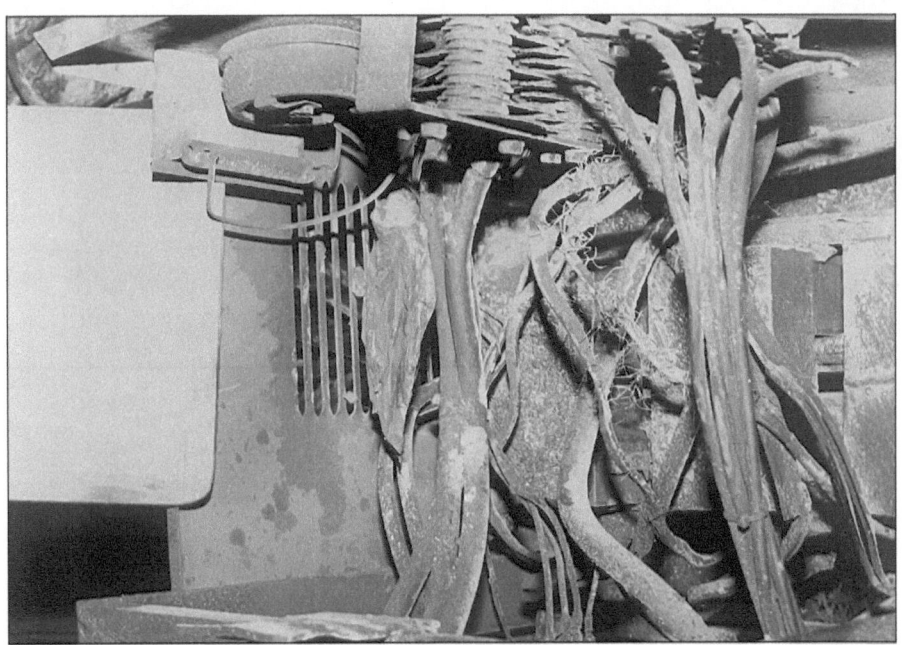

2 Left – welder

2 Left – right drive shuttle car

2 Left – left drive shuttle car

2 Left – fan tubing toward face

SS# 1924 – line battice

Personnel Carrier

Mounting Position of the Tachometer

Drive Motor Compartment

Test Instrumentation

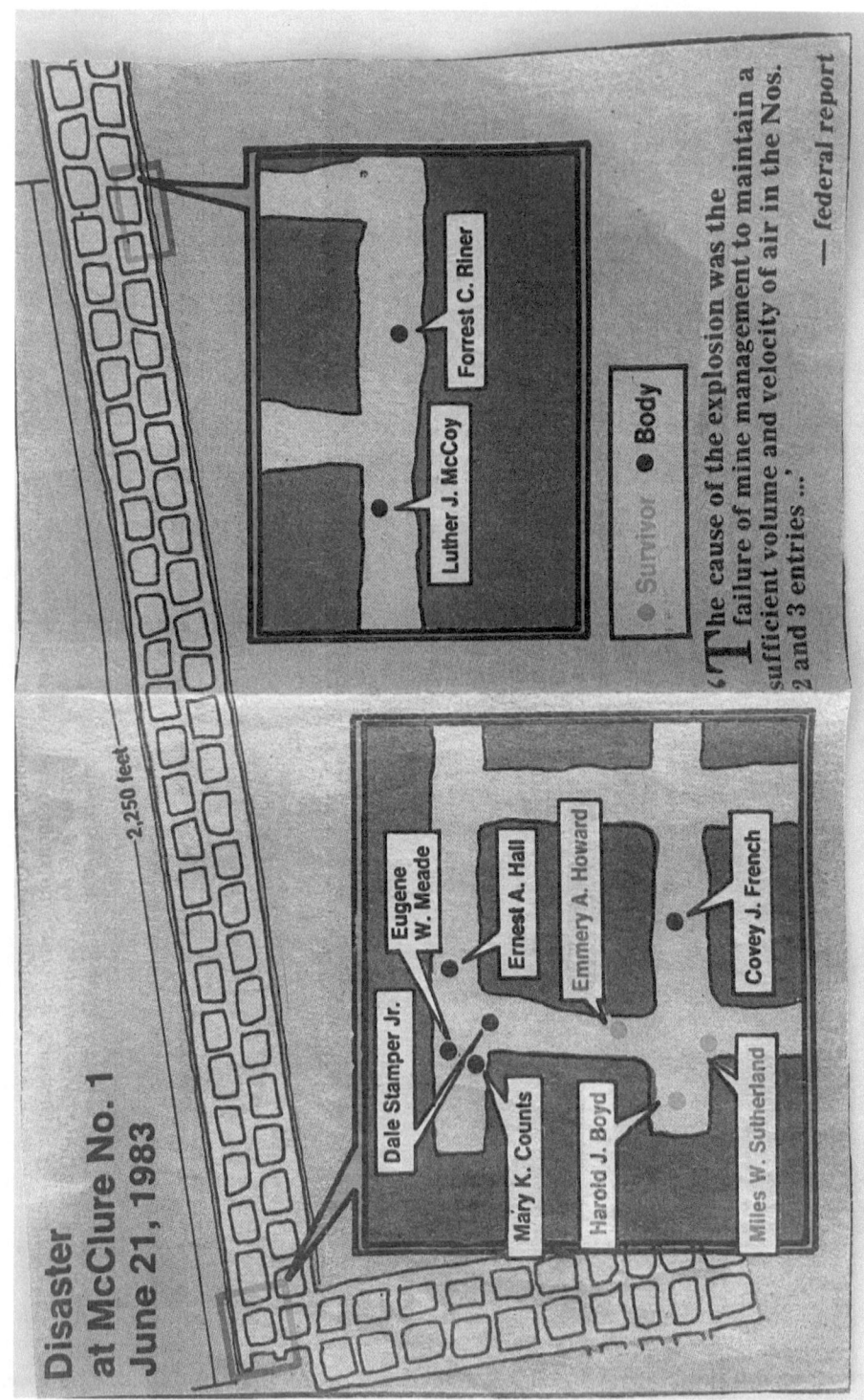

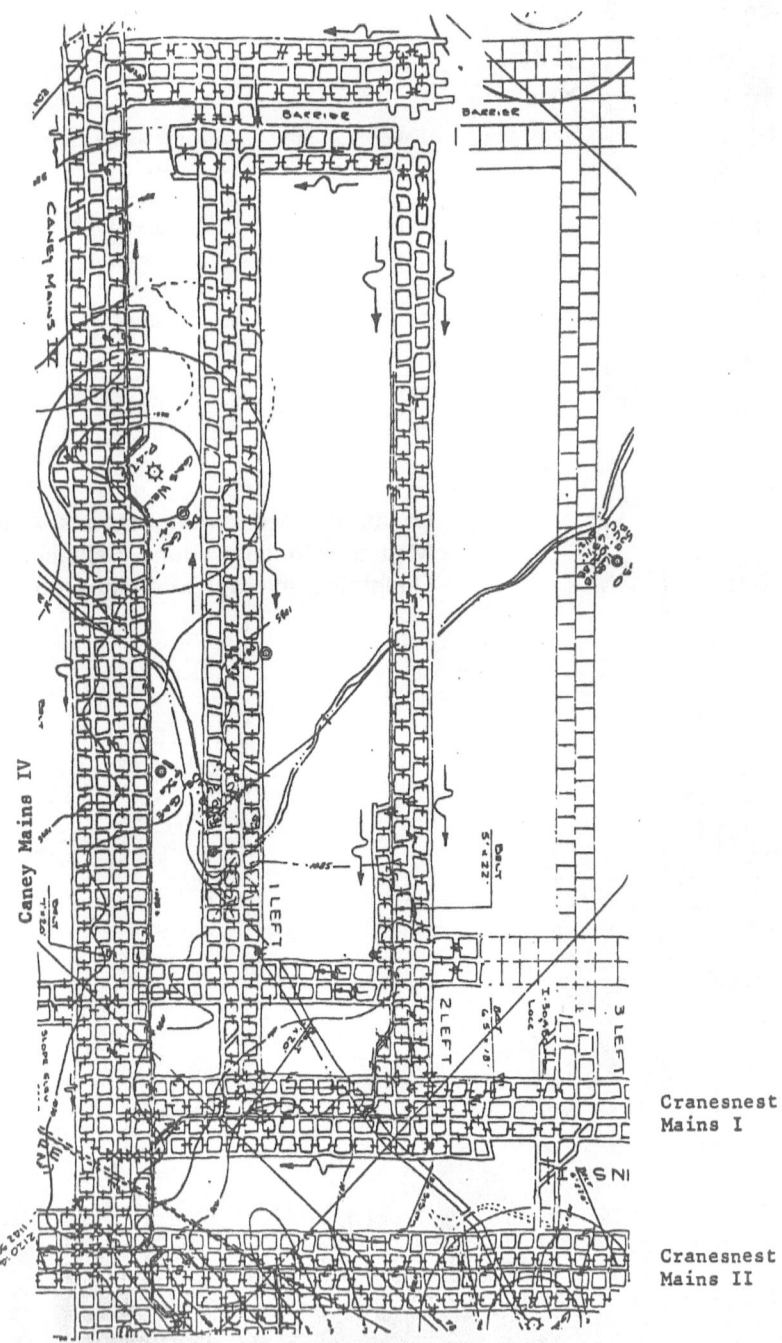

Survey Area, McClure No. 1 Mine

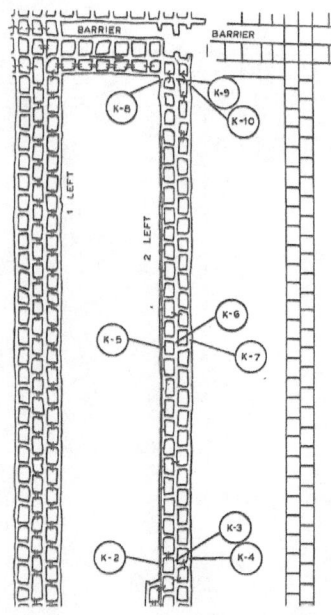

Location	Average methane conc. %	Balanced air quantity (cfm)	Average methane quantity (cfm)
K-2	0.61	10,000	61
K-3	0.24	6,000	14
K-4	0.47	28,000	132
K-5	0.48	18,000	86
K-6	0.27	6,000	16
K-7	0.40	20,000	80
K-8	0.08	25,000	20
K-9	0.13	9,000	12
K-10	0.22	10,000	22

Location of Monitoring Stations, Average Methane Concentrations, Balanced Air Quantities, Average Methane Quantities

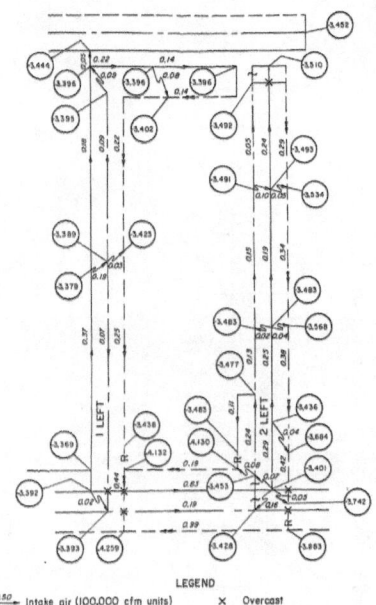

Ventilation Schematic of 2 Left Area Before Cut-through

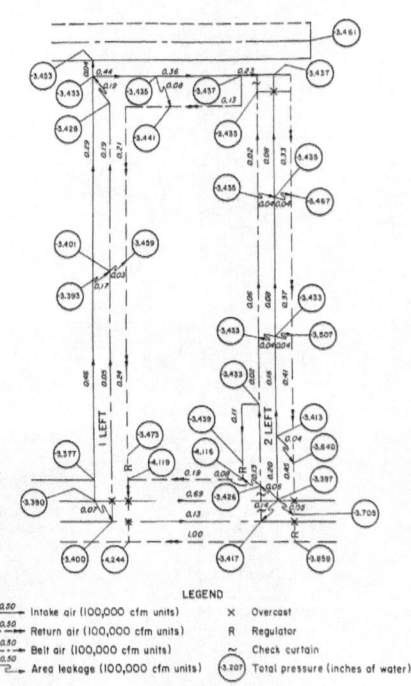

Ventilation Schematic of the Computer Simulation of 2 Left Area After Cut-through

9

"We're Going In!"

Darrell Holbrook

Darrell Holbrook

"We decided to ride up one Left to see if we could get back to the to-do list. Section 1 Left took us back to the bleeders I had previously walked into, and we had to walk across the face. Once we got there, we crossed the face and were probably within two or three crosscuts of 2 Left when we heard Miles hollering for help. At that moment, we knew we had at least one survivor. We knew his voice. I had known Miles for so many years, and we had worked together in different mines throughout our coal mining history.

"We crossed over and found Miles standing beside the roof bolter. We also discovered the other operator, Boyd, lying unconscious underneath the T-Bar. Emmery Howard was there, too, more or less in shock, crawling around trying to find his way. None of them had light; they were in total darkness.

"All their lights and hard hats had been blown off, so they couldn't see anything. And, of course, the dust was still thick throughout the mine. Before we reached Miles, we found Covey French, who had landed face down. He was already dead; rigor mortis had set in. When I turned him over, everything turned with him. We continued searching Section 2 Left, basically, in the same shape, except for those survivors. Then, once we got to looking around and saw what we had, it was evident. There had been an explosion on Section 2 Left.

"Miles was burned so badly that we couldn't calm him down; he wouldn't sit or lay down on a gurney. I hadn't realized the extent of his injuries. While we looked for others, Miles kept getting up, hollering, screaming, and praying for his crew.

"We decided that Blake and Ron should take Miles outside since he could walk. They helped him across the face to get some assistance. I stayed up with the other two; one unconscious and the other in shock. I had fresh air at the mouth of Section 1 Left, so I felt I could get them to safety if necessary.

"When Blake Blackstone returned, he said, 'I counted the hats. Hey, we've got five hats.' We had four people and started searching for the fifth. We were sure Riner and the repairman had been on the mantrip jeep we found at the mouth of the section. Realizing the fifth person was still on the section, we began our search.

"Eventually, we found the fifth one underneath some tubing beside the miner. We accounted for everyone except for the two guys that were on the mantrip. Once we got the last two survivors to the elevator, we went outside where the mine rescue team had already gathered. There were a couple of rescue teams at the bottom of the slope.

"Homer Wayne Fields, a mine rescuer, was among the first to start bringing out the bodies as they were found. When I reached the top of the elevator, they took me into the Superintendent's office — basically the headquarters at that time — and began to debrief me about what I had seen, what I had done, and what we needed to do next.

"After a brief conversation, they started sending the mine rescue team up to Section 2 Left. It wasn't long before they shouted back, 'We found them.'"

There was no communication from inside to the surface after the explosion, so they had to wait for someone to come outside and report what had actually happened.

"The next month or so was pretty tough. We spent most of our time recovering the mine, which was challenging for the crews we could bring in. We could only work eight or nine men at a time, and it was hard on them because they knew what had happened even though they hadn't witnessed it. I had been there the whole time and could see where we had made a difference and where things were improving.

"But those guys didn't know; they only had what they were told or what they saw on TV and in the newspapers. A lot of that wasn't true and didn't match what had actually happened. And, of course, we had the families who lost loved ones and friends. It was difficult for everyone, but I think it was much harder for them than for me. Not that I'm tougher, but I was right there for everything while they had to walk into a lot more unknowns than I did.

"The elevator ride down to the mine was quick, but I can't recall the exact time it took. I know that when Miles was working on Section 2 Left with Riner, McCoy, French, Counts, Howard, Boyd, Hall, and Stamper, they heard something unusual. They described it as a 'poof' that echoed twice.

"Ernie Hall survived briefly because he fell into water during the explosion. When it happened, it blew their hats off. Joe Boyd fell face-first into the dirt, leaving everyone to believe he was dead. Emmery Howard was disoriented, running around in shock, thinking someone had jumped on him. When we crossed the longwall face, about halfway, we could hear Miles. That's when we knew there was at least one survivor. Emmery was more in shock than anything else, not fully grasping what had occurred, while Boyd remained unconscious.

"I remember Sutherland being burned more severely than I realized. He was standing, and we kept trying to get him to lay down. I could feel the crispness of his coveralls, but I had no idea of the severity of his injuries at that moment. He would get back up, driven by his miner's bond instinct to help his fallen brothers.

"We were also looking for Blake Blackstone. When I reached out to touch the mantrip, it was hot, which indicated something was seriously wrong. We were already aware that an incident had occurred long before that moment.

"As I walked along, I began to see things like self-rescuers. The yellow markings became visible as the dust broke apart. Before that, we hadn't had any inspections or visits from MSHA, so there was a lot that hadn't been disturbed, which made spotting things a bit easier later on.

"The crews had a designated spot for laying down their self-rescuers, but as the section advanced, that location changed. Initially, we may have left them in one area, but as we moved forward, it wasn't easy to locate them again. There could have been signs indicating where they were, but they were buried under dust. Eventually, after the humidity helped break things up, I found them piled against the rib, identifiable by the little yellow markings.

"When the explosion happened, I was on another section, about 1,200 to 1,400 feet away, and it sounded like a massive airliner breaking apart. You could hear it long before you saw anything. I rushed outside to investigate. The area I was in was nearly as high as 10 feet, and the ventilation fly pads were pushed up against the roof by the force of the blast.

"The first wave brought up a cream-colored cloud, but it quickly turned dark with rock dust. That initial surge suspended the fresh dust in the air, creating a scene of chaos. It was terrifying to witness, and the impact was felt far and wide throughout the mine. Working in the mine and underground gets in your blood. I mean, it does.

"I don't know how much of that stuff was recovered. But for the first few days after the explosion, you couldn't find anything. Everything was covered with a quarter of an inch of dust, maybe more. Just black. Well, the first time it come up there, it suspended that rock dust. The fresh dust that was out probably. And that's what prevented a secondary explosion. And then it sort of breathed and come back again. It wasn't another explosion.

"Same explosion. It just blowed it up, sucked it back, and blowed it again. And the second time, it had already suspended the rock dust. So, the second time, it's just black because it's coal. The second time was black, but all those critics that said that mine wasn't rock dusted, I wouldn't be here if it hadn't been.

"My opinion is, if we hadn't gone, they wouldn't have let the rescue team go back for who knows how long. Somebody had to make the decision to go in. Well, this was bigger than anything that ever happened here in the mining in this area. Well, they came in and made a big — you know, they inspected there for, I don't know, what, a month? Six weeks? Anyway, after they did all that inspection.

"Yeah. And they did all that, and once they got through doing what they was inspecting, they decided they was going to inspect the mines. And I forget how many; they wrote 100 and some citations. And they was all a bunch of junk. A whole lot of them. One example that I know — see, we weren't supposed to change anything during that time. Well, on the section that I was running at the time, the curtain was hung up to where it was supposed to be legally.

"Well, during that four weeks, or whatever, end of that curtain fell down. You wasn't supposed to put it back, so they come along and they wrote a citation for that like it was down during the explosion. And there wasn't any way in the world they could — all those citations that they wrote wasn't there at the time of the explosion. I mean, if it blowed the curtain down during an explosion and then they come along later and write it up as the citation, sure, it's against the law.

"But anyway, they did a lot of that type stuff. There's one area up there that they'd cut crosscuts together right up in the face, and it was just a little hole. I mean, it might have been four or five feet wide and through it, it might have been five feet, but it wasn't bolted all the way. The bolt was probably like a foot of being in compliance.

"During the explosion, when we were doing all the inspection and all that, nobody noticed it. Everybody went through there because if you didn't go through there, you had to walk way around. Every inspector up there went through it. And then when they had the inspection, someone found it. Everybody had done it, but we got the citation like we were all up there doing that on a regular basis, but so were they.

"They should have went in there and said, 'This is what we need to do forward. This is going forward now.' I think I was involved with more of it than anyone. At least the ones living today. And now my way of looking at it — there might have been a mistake made here and there, but nobody intentionally made a mistake that caused it.

"And once it happened, I think there was a lot of people stepped up and did what they could to take care of people, but some, I believe, thought, 'A coal miner gets up every morning, and who can we cripple and kill today?'

"It didn't knock the fan out. The air was circulating and by the time we got back to the fan, which I'm going to guess was 40 minutes or so, it wasn't that long. But when I left my section, we stopped down there and looked up that longwall face because there's two of them had cut through and blowed the doors out. That's what saved my crew when it blew them out; I'm guessing it short circuited and most of the carbon monoxide went out that way.

"But there was some dust and stuff coming out then, but when we went back, there was still dust in the air in those areas. On 2 Left on the track going up there, that area didn't have as much pressure in the air. The dust was moving slower. That's why we seen it down there. It was still coming out there. And the reason it was traveling that way is that they had dropped an entry. There were four entries going up through there, and they dropped to Entry 1. Well, that became a return. It was a return before that, but it was regulated down.

"So, the air wasn't going out that entry as fast as it was everywhere else. And it was pulling all the air down that track entry. We would have never got back there wearing self-rescuers because they're too difficult to breathe through. See, they don't tell you that until you actually have an explosion. They made that big deal that companies wasn't training everybody properly.

"The companies, that's after they went to the SCE, the improved version. But the training modular that they sent with you to train them by the company told you once you got them on to move out. Didn't say how hard it was going to be to breathe, and it is hard. If you've ever put one on and try it, it's a job just to sit and breathe.

"And those guys, what they done, they put it on and did everything they was trained to do, but when they couldn't get no air, what are you going to do? You're going to raise it up.

"The telephone wire that went to the section melted off. There were pieces of brattice cloth that was hanging. There was also an old paintbrush that you'd paint your centers with. It was stuck up over a roof bolt plate. The bristles were burned off. Those curtains were, if I remember right, they was probably on that longwall face, but they were doubled. It's not just the one; there were several of them doubled up. This is probably just one that the heat melted. The heat hit them and the plastic-like stuff just run off of it, and some places it actually burned.

"We kept telling Sutherland to calm down. I remember that pinner had a cushion in it. We got that cushion and tried to get him to lay down on that cushion and rest, but he wasn't going to have that.

"I was shocked to find out that he was burnt as bad as he was. He was just black then. It was just sheath coming off. The coveralls he had on were in his back. The imprint even was still in his back. Sutherland wasn't as black as the rest of them because he was up in that little nook where the vent was at, out away from some of the dust. But I was really surprised that he was that bad off.

"Emmery had huge blisters from below his eyes down his chin. Joe, it blew him up against the top first and took his cap and light off and then face forward and knocked him unconscious, so he didn't raise up.

"I thought he was probably the worst one of them as far as being hurt. I thought Joe was probably in worse shape because he was unconscious. Can't get a good man down like Miles, now. He ain't getting down. He said, 'They kept trying to lay me down to rest,' and he said, 'I ain't laying down for nothing.'"

10

RESCUE & RECOVERY

Ron Sluss

Sluss was a young man of 31 years of age when the explosion happened. He had 10 years of mining experience. It took a big part of his time to get things where they needed to go. He went underground about 5:00 p.m. and went to the Crane's Nest 3 and then adjacent to it, Crane's Nest 4. They were working on collars. He was an Assistant Mine Foreman on the evening shift.

Sluss got on a jeep and went to Section 2 Left about 7:00 p.m. "As soon as I got there, a drive chain broke on a feeder. After seeing that it was worn, we decided to put a new one on. We were looking at that, trying to get the guards off. A few minutes later, here come Johnny Steel and F.C. Riner.

"I hit my head on an overhanging wire there near the supply house and got bumped against my hat at the very instant you could feel the waves. One of the double-air lock doors was blown open, which took some force. And with that commotion, everybody was wondering, 'What in the hell happened?'

"I thought it was a rockfall right next to the fan or the intake shaft next to the elevator to make that shock wave. I just felt one shock wave. I started hollering for Eddie Glovier, the Maintenance Foreman, to check the fan because I knew it would read in the water gauge. The water gauge was running close to eight inches and dropped back down to five inches and shot right back up. Then everything leveled up. I'm doing everything I can to get in touch with the sections. Something major has happened. What could it be?

"At this point, people start coming out of the mine. All the miners were asked what had happened and nobody could answer. They had felt something shake the earth and started heading out of the mine. They didn't have a clue that the mine had just blew. We got in contact with every section except Section 2 Left crew. Darrell Holbrook was the Foreman on Caney 4 and told me about all the smoke, dust, and debris that he had to come through. And by now, they knew there had definitely been an ignition somewhere."

Sluss asked Darrell, "Will you go back in with me to check it?" Holbrook said, "Yeah. Let's make sure our rescuers are good and everything." At that time, Roy Glover was told to kill the power in the mine. Total darkness followed.

Sluss and Holbrook went on to Section 2 Left. When they

got to the mouth of Section 2 Left, they came up on the mantrip jeep. "I seen how hot it was and how it was scorched. I thought at that time it had blown up from the section. I didn't realize. There was clean fresh air around the jeep, even though it looked burned. It was black and hot. It was hot. So hot that you could not lay your hand on it for very long. We found the jeep. It was heading toward the outside.

"The only thing we seen from the men was that one boot without the strings. We thought it had been there before because we had discussed it. The boot wasn't burned, but there were no strings in it. They had melted. There was so much thick smoke, it was hard to breathe. As we slowly made our way up to Section 2, we had to remove debris off the track and check the methane gas readings as we moved forward."

Blake Blackstone joined Sluss and Holbrook and continued forward on foot. All of a sudden, they heard a voice. They recognized it immediately. It was Miles Sutherland. "I knew Miles. I knew his voice instantly. It was Miles hollering. Blake and I went on to Miles. He was standing, looking toward the face to the left of the roof bolter. He was standing up with his hands on the roof bolter talking to us.

"Of course, he was coming and going. He wasn't sure exactly where he was at or what happened. He knew he had been in an explosion. He said, 'We blowed up, boys.' I told him, 'Yeah.' And then he prayed, and I prayed with him, trying to keep him settled down. At the time, Blake stayed with Miles, and Darrell checked the pulse of Joe Boyd, the other roof bolter operator. He was on the ground unconscious.

"Darrell said there was a pulse, but his breathing was irregular and erratic. He was having trouble breathing. I seen Emmery sitting, and I went over to him. He was talking, but he really wasn't saying nothing. He was very out of it and talking out of his head. He wasn't sure exactly where he was. Boyd was found at the front of his pinner head. He was laying on his right side. I went to Howard, Darrell went to Joe, and Blake was still with Miles.

"We found Howard at Crosscut 40. He was moving. He was breathing good, but I could not understand a word he was saying. I didn't know if he would get worse, but at that time, he was breathing. He was burned. The skin was rolling off his hand, his nose, and ears.

"At that point, I continued on across Crosscut 40. The first lifeless body we found was Ernest Hall. He was laying face down. I turned him over. I took a carotid check for a pulse. At the same time, Darrell took one on his wrist. We found nothing. Ernie's face was underwater. It was under watery coal, like where a continuous miner had been running. His face was wet, is the reason he wasn't burned. He wasn't burned at all in the face.

"Darrell checked Dale Stamper next. I didn't assist in checking Stamper. He checked him while I was laying Hall back down. I had rolled him up to check him. Then both of us found Eugene Meade, who was a very heavy man, and pulled him some out from the underneath the boom of the continuous miner to check him. And then, of course, we found nothing. There was no pulse.

"I was searching and looking and hollering for any voices or sounds of life. No one answered. I knew at the time F.C. Riner and Mary Counts hadn't been found. I was trying to find them. It was so dark you couldn't see your hand in front of your face. You could feel, but everything was different. The explosion had changed everything we knew as it was previously.

"We came back before the dinner hole, and we walked up toward where Blackstone was at with Sutherland and decided we had to have some help to get them out. I asked Blake to stay with Howard and Boyd while I took Sutherland outside. Blackstone and I got Sutherland under each arm and walked him out to the jeep, loaded him up, brought him out to the surface.

"We had to walk with Sutherland. He couldn't sit or lay down. It was so dusty, and our mouths got so dry that we couldn't even spit. We just didn't realize how badly Sutherland had been injured and what degree of burns he had all over his body. As we would learn later, it was extensive. He had third-degree burns over 67 percent of his body. It was so dark, we couldn't see his face and how burned it was. Half of his ear was gone.

"There was smoke, but didn't see any blaze. It was smoke coming from the welder. It was still running. And maybe some smoke coming from the current, but those are the only too small... just smoke. No blaze. No fire."

As Sluss was driving the jeep, Blackstone was holding onto Sutherland as they made their way out of the mine.

"We got to the bottom of the elevator. Kellis Barton helped us get Sutherland onto the elevator and up the elevator. As soon as we got Sutherland outside, we put him into the Clinchfield ambulance. It had been pulled out and ready to take Sutherland. Sammy Salyers ended up going with Sutherland. I told the Superintendent the best I could, 'We do have some dead. We do have some alive. There are survivors. There is fresh air. We can get to them.'

"We got our names together and recorded and went back underground, not knowing what we were going back into. There were several of us that went back down underground to search for our buddies. We have a bond. It's called the Coal Miner's Bond. We never leave one behind."[1]

Information in this chapter via public record.

Norman Lewis

His Story

Norman Lewis was born April 4, 1954, in Harlan, Kentucky. His dad Luther was a school teacher in Clintwood, Virginia, and his mom Mary Lou was a nurse at Park Avenue in Norton, Virginia, and for Public Health Service in Dickenson County.

Norman and Judy Large were married September 1, 1973, and have two children. A daughter named Jessica was born a month before the explosion in 1983. Their son Nicholas was born in 1992.

Lewis graduated from Clinch Valley College in 1997 with a bachelor's degree. He started working at McClure #1 Mine as Day Shift Mine Examiner in June of '79 and helped to develop the mine after Thyssen Mining from Germany had dropped the shaft.

Lewis was also the captain of the McClure #1 Mine rescue team once it was developed.

"I was on Section 2 Left on Wednesday before the explosion that occurred on June 21, 1983. The section was idle for maintenance. Everything was normal," Lewis said.

"That Tuesday night, I was at home between 10:30 and 10:45 p.m. I got a call from James Stapleton, the mobile equipment operator evening shift. He was screaming at the top of his lungs, 'Get your rescue team together and get them to the mine.' I said, 'Duck, what happened?' He said, 'Oh, Lord, they've blowed it up! They've blowed it up! Get your team, get down here. They've blowed it up!' I said, 'Slow down. What?' And he started explaining to me. I said, 'Well, I'll be on my way.' I immediately left for the mine. I didn't tell Judy anything was going on.

"On my way to the mine, when I turned at the bridge in Fremont, two to three miles away from the access road of the mine, I could smell burning sulfur and diesel fuel. Right as you came in the gate is where the mine fan was. You went back and it was running, but it looked like you had a black curtain coming out of that funnel off the fan. It's a 10-foot fan. And going straight up into the sky. I knew the fan was operating.

"I started taking the phone numbers from the file and calling each one on the rescue team. I informed Donald Duncan, Marquis Neece, and Lee Ratliff. At that time, we were unable to get in touch with Bo Willis, Steve Hale, and John Brooks. The local sheriff departments helped us to get in touch with them.

"We geared up and started going in. Sluss and Blackstone were bringing Sutherland out of the mine as I was going to get my light. A tremendous gang of people had gathered round. They were coming off the elevator, and they were coming on for the next shift, and everybody was just standing there in shock.

"Twelve of us jumped into mantrip jeeps and took off heading in. Once we got to the section, we decided not to go to 2 Left, so we went in 1 Left and go across the setup entries where the longwall was going to be, because they told us there were two more men alive on the section.

"As soon as we got off the jeep, we took checks. As we were walking across the long wall, we were in a hurry. We only had one stretcher and medical items. With the amount of burns the miners could possibly have, I didn't think we could do them that much good. We were scared.

"It felt like my Adam's apple was in the back of my mouth. A human rescue man actually will crawl into the barrel of a cannon, and it loaded to try to save somebody's life. And that's what we were doing. We had no idea. It was hot. I mean, physically hot. When we got off that mantrip jeep, we were close to 1,000 feet away from that section, and the atmosphere was hot.

"There was no smell to it. We didn't have any detection device. I had my methane reader. That's all we had. Some of us had started running, and I told them, 'We've got to slow down. We don't know what we're running into, carbon monoxide or oxygen. We've got to get there, but we've got to be alive when we get there.'

"As coal miners, we're used to going into those sections, and it's like being in a house that's painted white 'cause the rock dust has covered all the sides and ceilings. The miners of 2 Left had no hats on. They had been blown off and it was total darkness. On 2 Left, we walked up that entry and came around the corner and found Covey French laying in the middle of the haul way with his head toward the right rib. I didn't recognize him. I stopped to check French and, of course, I didn't know who it was. I couldn't tell.

"And I looked at his belt tag, and I could tell by that time there was no life. I went on toward the face. When we got to the face of the 3 Entry on 2 Left where the roof bolter was, they brought Howard through the curtains leading to 4 Entry to me and Lee Ratliff and said, 'We need to get him out.' And the other people went to Joe Boyd, who was in front of the roof bolter on the right side and started putting him on the backboard.

"Out of the darkness, a set of hands comes at me with a bloodcurdling scream: 'Don't leave me in the dark! Don't leave me alone.' It was Emmery Howard. As nature would have it, I reached out and grabbed those arms. It burst the blisters on his arms where he was burnt. I'll never forget that. I'll never forget that feeling when he said, 'Don't leave me. Don't leave.' I said, 'I'm not going to leave you. We're going to take you with us.'

But he wouldn't turn loose of me.

"He told us he was thirsty, extremely thirsty. I moved a box of water sitting on top of the roof bolter to the operator's deck. And about that time, another scream came from in front of me. It was so dark from the soot and the dust that we couldn't see anything. It was like we didn't even have a light on. He knew us when we got to him.

"I handed the water to Howard and told him, 'Just wash your mouth out and get the taste out of your mouth. Drink slowly.' He had significant burns on his face, neck, and arms. He seemed to know where everybody was on the section. I asked him about Covey. Howard said, 'Covey went to get the rescuers, and he never did come back. We had all been at the miner hanging ventilation tubing when the flame path came through the section to us.'

"Howard told us that he had heard Cat making noises. He said, 'I don't think she made it.' I told him, 'I'm glad to see you're alive.' He said, 'You all are the best thing we've seen, so we enjoy seeing you all.' I said, 'We're going to have to get you out of here, and we want to carry you.'

"Howard wouldn't let us carry him, saying, 'I can walk out.' He was in shock, trembling and shaking. I told him again, 'We need to carry you,' and he wouldn't hear of it. He said, 'I've got to walk out of here.' And the way we had to bring him out was down 3 Entry. We walked him by French, and I turned to try to block where he couldn't see him laying there, and he told me, 'Covey is laying right there.' So, we just walked by and our lights never did shine on him, but he knew where people were.

"By the time we got Howard to the mantrip on 1 Left, they already had Boyd on the backboard and carried him over there. Marquis Neece, an EMT on the Rescue Team, he went with James Vernon Stanley on the Dante Team for Clinchfield Coal and took them to the elevator. Ratliff and I turned and went back to the section. By that time, they were trying to locate Riner and McCoy. At that time, the section was quite warm, and we had smoke and dust all across the section.

"After bringing Howard out, I went back on the mantrip to the bottom of the elevator, and I met Tom Asbury, captain of the Dante mine rescue team. He had six or seven members there with their equipment on ready to go to Section 2 Left. Not long after going back in, Bo Willis hollered, 'I've got a body.' Not long after that, I heard them call that they had the second body. So, we went to pick the bodies up as they explored further on.

"We brought Riner out first, then we brought McCoy. We carried them all the way back to where the jeep was parked at the flies at the mouth of the section. Then they brought the jeeps up after that. They brought the jeeps up and took those two bodies out. After they left with those two bodies, they decided to try to speed up the examination of the area. We took different entries and checked for methane and carbon monoxide. The most that was found was a trace of carbon monoxide and seven-tenths methane.

"At one place in the 4 Entry, we found a water hole that was so large we couldn't wade it. It was about two break lengths long. We came to the 3 Entry and went around and went straight back into 4 as quick as we could. We waded up to almost over our boot tops to get back into 4.

"We encountered one more water hole up closer to the face. Instead of trying to go around it, we waded it. It was waist deep. We continued our way throughout the mine checking brattices. As I was walking by the battery station, I remember looking at the batteries because that's the first thing we did when we got to that break. We stopped and made a carbon monoxide check. I said, 'Let's check the batteries. We're in the battery charging station.' I believe one set had connectors in them. The lids were off the batteries. There didn't seem to be a lot of damage there. Of course, everything was black. Everything down the entry was black. I can't remember exactly whether the charger was hooked into them or not.

"The rest of my team came in and some of the foremen for the third shift with jeeps and was going to remove the bodies. Asbury said, 'You all come back down and sit down, let's take a break. These people are fresh. We'll let them pick up what they can or pick up the bodies, and if they need our help to carry them, we'll go back.'

"So, we went to the tailpiece and sat down on the belt structure right there and rested for a few minutes. They started bringing the first body to the end of the track. We went up and helped them walk down the feeder. The supply cars were parked at the feeder, making it tight to carry a stretcher through that area. You had to turn sideways.

"We still had our Draeger ventilators on our backs. And we'd get together two or three of us at a time and try to hand-walk the body by, and we'd take it and put it on the jeep, go back, and get the other. After they got the bodies loaded, I got on the jeep, which was the 2 Left Section jeep. I noticed it had a lot of dust on it and was black. They started out on mantrip jeeps and got halfway off the section, and one of the jeeps came off the rail.

"We had to try to get it on. We worked 15 or 20 minutes trying to get the mantrip back on. It seemed like there were three mantrips, and the ones that had battery power weren't very good. We pushed the other jeeps off the section after they got them back on track.

"When we came up the hill coming toward the elevator, the other jeeps just wouldn't do it, and we pushed them up that hill also, that same hill with the same jeep. We came to the elevator bottom. The first crews that were there went out with the bodies — with three of the bodies and the crew I was with. We brought two bodies, Riner and McCoy, up with us as we came on the last trip out.

"Approximately, 84 workers were underground at 10:15 p.m. when the blast occurred. Of the 84, 74 came to the surface uninjured. 10 miners were working in the accident area at the time of the explosion. Recovery was complete at 5:30 a.m.

"Once I got into working underground, I loved it. I loved the smell, I loved the camaraderie, and the jokes. In all mines, jokesters and people do things like that, making a lot of things, but you have to. It was to break the tension. People in combat would do things like that. Just anything to ease the tension.

"The siren of the deep caused us to want to go, and we were productive. We were polishing the Clinchfield Jewel. These miners are a brotherhood, and all worked closely together and lived near each other all their lives. They were family."

Homer Wayne Fields

His Story

Homer Wayne Fields was born to Homer and Florence Fields of Dante, Virginia. His dad worked for Clinchfield for 41 years. He has three siblings: Norm Lee, Kay, and Jenny, who is now deceased. He is married to Kimberly Kelly and lives in Castlewood, Virginia. Wayne has two daughters, Terra and Alexandria.

He began working for Clinchfield Coal Company on February 4, 1974, and retired September 9, 1995.

At the time of the explosion, Fields had been a member of Dante mine rescue team. He played a crucial part in the search and recovery of two other mine explosions; Scotia and the P&P at St. Charles, Virginia.

Fields worked in the Safety Department and was assigned to McClure #1 for over two and half years. During the years, he did various jobs: roof bolter, wireman, and laying track, among other responsibilities.

"When I do an inspection, I always walk in and follow the belt line to the section I'm going to," he said. "I personally check all the equipment and cables. If the section is idle, I check everything on it. I check all the ribs, roof, and ventilation.

"As I recall, I had not been in McClure #1 since June 9 for a short time. At that time, they had not cut into 1 Left on the longwall face. I checked there for gas, and it was just starting a fresh cut, and the air would knock you down, so I didn't take an air reading. I wasn't worried about it. If methane accumulation is found above one percent, it is taken care of right then. I do not leave the section until that is corrected.

"I went underground on the 21st to the Caney 4 Section with a federal inspector, Gerald Sloce, and the union representative, Sam Clay. We were able to hear the miner running on 2 Left, but we weren't in that area.

"When Caney 4 cut into 1 Left, we talked about it as soon as it cut through to be curtained off. We would usually put up a curtain board before we cut in. Then once we cut into the area and the continuous backed out, we let the pinner go in and hang curtain up behind. The pinner would finish bolting the place and pull out of it. And when it pulled out, the scoop would go in and clean it up, and then the curtain was left in place.

"There were incidents prior to the explosion on the 21st where methane had been detected in the corner of the Dogleg, and I did find seven percent right in the corner. It was just in the left corner of the face. Randy Beverly and I cleared it out right then. We hung a curtain in it and after that, it went down to three-tenths. It cleared up to zero.

"We were staying shut down constantly with the gas running over the one percent. The continuous miner would shut off regularly when the gas reached over one percent. The mine is gassy like that — you know, it's not a crime to have gas. It's a crime to walk off and leave it. If it's over one percent, we automatically — we instantly clean it out. When we encounter elevated gas, we always have two evils to fight; you either eat dust a little bit one time or have a dead pocket of gas at the face. We chose not to have the dead pocket of gas because when we cut into the air, the dust blew back onto the miners.

"At 10:45 p.m. on the night of the accident, Wayne Hamilton, the supply man, notified me at home. He told me they had either had an explosion or a big roof fall. Something interrupted the ventilation, and they could not get a hold of the 2 Left crew. And I told him to keep trying to get a hold of the 2 Left Crew and I would notify the rest of the mine rescue crew, and we'd be there immediately.

"After I hung up talking to him, I called Tom Asbury. I informed him what I had heard, and I was going to the mine, and have his wife get ahold of the rest of the crew. So, I went straight to the Training Center to get his apparatus. And on the way, I stopped at Junior Leonard's. I blew the horn and got him to go with me to load the equipment.

"When I got over there, I cut the lock on the door and went in. I believe it was seven machines, a carbon monoxide detector, oxygen indicators and our extra methane spotters, and I left with them.

"So, let's start with the elevator going down into the intake shaft. And then you've got the mantrip jeep, is what they went down in, because actual air went down it, too. But we had two doors at the bottom to try to block it off. It was a big, round-like tube, but it's concrete. And one-half of it, that was where the fresh air did go into the mine at, and then it came down, and it branched off into the intakes, which the trackway was not in the intakes.

"The fan for McClure #1 Mine was at Fremont going toward Clintwood. It was just right down the road below it right there, about not much more than 1,000 feet from the intake shaft. Because it actually, you know, there's a big hole in the ground that you pulled air up out of the ground with. The crew for that Section usually went down the shaft together. They were altogether when they went down, but there would have probably been more men, too.

"Miles always had his Bible. He kept it in his shirt pocket. He had always bragged to us that his daughter had given it to him from quoting Bible verses at school. They'd have gotten on the mantrip jeep, and it would have taken them approximately a mile to actually get to Section 2 Left. You're like 400 feet under the earth. That was the depth of the elevator was 400 feet that we went down the shaft.

"When you get back into the mine, there is a huge mountain over top of you. So, when you're 800 feet underground and you travel another mile straight back into the mountain to the face of the mine, you are in the core of the Earth. You're not going down deep. You're going down 800 feet, and then you're going out a mile. You maybe go through a valley if you're 400 feet under the earth, but then a big mountain. You just keep going straight, and you could be even 1,000 feet under the earth.

"Well, what 2 Left did, they traveled down what we call Crane's Nest and then they went down and turned off of Crane's Nest 2 and went across over to Crane's Nest 1. And then it took you past 1 Left, and then the next one is 2 Left. And that's the one they went up. I have a map that shows me the feet and the distance and where each miner was at after the explosion. They said, 'One curtain was blown one way, and it tore it in half, and then the other half came back the other way.'

"It was approximately 11:45 p.m. when I got to the mine. Harry Childers met me at the parking lot because I came in sliding sideways. After immediately putting on my mine rescue apparatus, I went to the elevator because I had the carbon monoxide detector. When I started down the elevator, halfway down, Mike Wright, the owl shift superintendent, hollered and asked me not to go in by myself.

"I proceeded on to the bottom and got them some water. They were in need and wanting water badly. When I came back outside some of the rest of the mine rescue members had arrived. I took them back into the conference room and went over the ventilation and the escapeway off the 2 Left area, the 1 Left and the Caney 4 area. I was trying to brief them on the ways we were going back into the sections.

"By that time, Monroe West and Neil Phillips came back there, and we decided we were going to go to the mouth of 2 Left and proceed our way up, because we had two men missing.

"As we started to advance — the first mine rescue team was going inby — they found the telephone wires were melted together. At that point, we started disconnecting the belt control line and hooking it into our telephone approximately every three breaks. If there wasn't a plug there, we cut it in two. I had the pliers and cut them in two. We would strip them down and hook the phone up. Just before we got to the section, somebody outby stepped on our phone line and disconnected it, and Ray Robinette went back, found it, tied a knot in it, and put it back together.

"We had to tie two knots in the line, and we advanced on to the feeder. Then we all got together there at the Dogleg because we had come up on smoke, but it only had a trace of CO in it. By now, we had two rescue teams, and we started advancing ahead. One team would advance every three breaks, then the other team would advance up when it was clear. As we were going up, all of these brattices appeared to be okay, and as we came on up toward the area where we knew the Dogleg was, we started seeing the return — a door. I believe it was the first thing we saw blown out. Then we saw a couple of brattices that appeared to be out.

"When we got to the mouth of 2 Left, four people went up the number 2 Entry. Myself and Monroe and Bill Clemons went up the intake entry — the number 3 Entry up to the Dogleg area. When we got to that area, Riner and McCoy were found. I went up then to help pick them up. We examined them and marked them off the way they were there — took the belts off, identified them, and we carried them back down to the Dogleg area. They brought a jeep up and took those two bodies out.

"On the way out with the bodies, one of the jeeps went down. It ran out of power. We tried pushing it with another one — the one behind it — and we set the jeep off the track. I had gone on out and then I came back in with another jeep, and they had a jeep that had wrecked. I tied my jeep to the first one. The one the power was out of, and I pulled it to the elevator bottom. Then I helped carry the bodies over to the elevator and we took them up. They had fallen off of the jeep that had become disabled.

"We helped load them into the ambulances and that was pretty well it. They called us back into the room. Back there,

Monroe West and Mr. Clemons gave us a little talk on what we had done, commended us on our work. That was somewhere around 5:30 a.m. on Wednesday the 22nd.

"See what happens, if you could just imagine. The pressure went toward the faces. You know, once it gets up, goes up through there, your pressure equalizes because it's just like blowing into a pop bottle. You blow into it but then, you know, once it hits the back, what air is in there...it equalizes out right there and stops. Well, the fire went on, but the pressure from the explosion kind of stopped just right next to Miles and Joe, because Joe had fell down. You know, that's what kept Joe from getting burned. And Miles was still standing up. He covered his eyes with his hands, was the only thing that saved his eyesight.

"And they kept trying to lay him down, and he wouldn't lay down on the gurney. He wouldn't lay down, and it was because his back was burned so badly, and what we didn't realize was his coveralls were melted into the back of his body.

"The air was really not moving. And that's what let the gas build up. Ventilation was actually coming up the 2 Entry, but it wasn't coming up the 1 Entry like where the jeep was at. There was ventilation up there, which fooled up everybody because the air was up there, but it wasn't going back down the return like it ought to have. It was going back and going down one less return. And that's what had let the gas build up in that number 1 Entry. That's the number 1 Entry of Section 2 Left. And when they started back down in the jeep, they got about halfway down, and that's when they ignited the methane. And I'm not blaming them or nothing.

"As far as F.C. Riner and McCoy, they were blown off the jeep. They were laying partly under the belt. And they were burnt pretty bad, but not real bad. But it actually blew their boots off of their feet. When you have an explosion right where it's at, you have the least violence there, but the pressure is what got them because see, it went toward the face and then went back toward the outside. It was just that sudden percussion right at them that did that to them.

"Miles said he felt pressure. He felt it. He felt something and knew something was happening, and Miles turned around and he saw it coming. That whole wall of fire was coming toward Miles and Joe. Miles had just enough time to put his hands over his eyes. It knocked Joe out. He was unconscious. We thought he was dead. Passed by him twice.

"At the time of the explosion, I was salary, but I got along with everybody. We are family. We spent so much time together and had for years. I just want to know what happened. There was another boy that survived up there, Emmery Howard. F.C. Riner had fired him. Riner felt so bad. It bothered him that he had to fire him because Riner knew he had five kids at home to feed. So, a short time later, he hired Emmery back.

"But then, see, it didn't kill Ernie Hall either. And there was a Meade boy. But they went back trying to get to their rescuers, you know, and the carbon monoxide is what killed them.

"Miles and Joe were already outside when I got there to go underground. All I remember hearing when I got there was, 'This is Darrell Holbrook, and I am outside.' He was calling over the radio. Miles was already out of the mine and was standing there yelling and hollering in pain. They were trying to help him get his coveralls off, and he was just screaming, 'You've got to stop.' And they're like, 'We've got to get these clothes off you.' And he said, 'They're stuck to me! They're melted to me!'

"The sad part of it is, I envisioned all of that because I'd been there so many times. Some of us took stretchers and carried them out of there…I'd say 1,500 feet, probably, back to where the curve went up into 2 Left, and then we loaded them on the jeep. And we moved probably 50 feet, and the jeep wrecked.

"And Ray Robinette went to cussing like crazy. So, we jacked the jeep back up and looked around, and there was Ray on his knees saying, 'Lord, forgive me. I'm so sorry that I said anything.' And I said, 'You know, you've done cussed the Lord, and you're going to be alright asking for forgiveness,' and that's with two dead bodies on the jeep that we were trying to get outside. That was hard.

"The other two miners were recovered around 12:30 a.m. Rescue team members had expected to find McCoy, Counts, and Riner in Section 2 Left. Counts was discovered shortly after with a piece of curtain material found near the left side of the continuous mining machine. I did observe Riner and

McCoy. Those are the only two I saw because I didn't want to look at the other people, because I knew them.

"Mr. Riner was on his hands and knees, pulled up in a knot, kind of, with his head back in toward his knees. He was against the rail. He was kind of charcoaled. I guess what you would say, burned. One of his boots was completely missing. The other boot, from his heel up toward his leg, was still there. The toe part was missing. His fingers were kind of like they were webbed, and he had no hair. That's pretty well all I can remember about him.

"Mr. McCoy, he was laying down on his stomach, kind of like he was trying to go up under the belt line. I didn't look him right in the face, but he had just a sprig or two of hair, short pieces, up off the back of his neck. He had no hair on his head. His fingers were kind of webbed, and his clothes were burned. They were both severely burned.

"On the inby end of the mantrip jeep, there were charcoal-colored burns on it. The reflectors were burned to where you couldn't tell they were reflectors. On both sides, and on the outby end, had a little dust on them, but they were cleaned off and you could recognize them. The heat was so hot that the headrests of the jeep were melted down partly, not completely."

Fields had sketched the area on the brattices, and in that particular area, the brattices had blown over against the solid blocks from Number 2 over to Number 3. "The concrete blocks were over against the blocks of coal," he said. "Evidence of paper had blown over against the solid blocks and had came back on the end of the roof bolt plates toward the solid block. In that area, the brattices had tapered off. Some of them, the doors had blown out in them. And then inby, the block area, the blocks had just turned over."

He also recalls the area where Riner and McCoy were between 3 and 4. "There were several blocks blown down," he said. "Those locations were found much different than the remainder of them on Section 2 Left."

Fields still holds the belief that the accident area was right near where he found Riner and McCoy. "I feel that's where the accident area was."

Wayne and Kim Fields

Danny Mann

His Story

Danny Mann was part of the rescue team on the night of the explosion. He grew up in Dungannon, Virginia, married Kathy, and they have one daughter and two granddaughters. He started working for Clinchfield Coal Company in December 1974.

"I started working for Clinchfield in December 1974. I became a union coal miner September of 1981, and that's when I joined the mine rescue team. I took a job in safety and signed on at a couple of mines in Russell County: Wilder and Chaney Creek. They shut those mines down in 1982, so I went to the Splashdam Mine in Haysi. That's where I was working when the explosion happened at McClure.

"On that fateful night in 1983, I got the call after 10:15 p.m. We went to the station, got the truck, and prepared to head out. My brother Ronnie worked at McClure #1, and he had just signed on for a day shift motorman job. He had been working on Section 2 Left with Kathleen Counts, Sutherland, Howard, Boyd, and the rest of them.

"A few weeks before, Ronnie had signed off that section, and Cat, as we called Kathleen Counts, had taken his job. She was there when the explosion occurred. That night, I had a couple of years' experience of mine rescue, but this was my first actual mine event. When we arrived, we got our breathing apparatus and other rescue equipment. We were informed that three survivors — Emmery Howard, Miles Sutherland, and Joe Boyd — had already been brought out. Unfortunately, five workers were confirmed dead, and two others, F.C. Riner and Luther McCoy, were still missing.

"We went underground. We reached the Cranes Nest turn-off, where we encountered the remains of the mantrip that had been operating in the area but had since derailed. The tract was coated with soot, and the mantrip was obviously exposed to a massive amount of heat. From there, we proceeded toward Section 2 Left.

"We found the bodies of Riner and McCoy about 1,000 feet past the mantrip. I won't get into graphic details, but the burns were so severe that I couldn't recognize them. It was as if their skin had been scorched off, like when a marshmallow catches fire. F.C. had leather boots on, but they were blown off his feet. His feet were burned so badly that the skin was separated from the bottom of his feet. It was clear they were deceased, so we placed them in body bags.

"As we continued searching, we found the body of Cat (Kathleen Counts). She didn't die instantly. She had taken her hand and dug a hole in the coal, like trying to protect herself from the explosion. I identified her by the name tag on her belt and wrote her name on the body bag. The whole operation didn't take as long as it might seem, but we had to walk 5,000 feet from where our mantrip trip had been to reach the section where the explosion had occurred.

"At the time, time didn't matter much. I got the call after 10:15 p.m. By the time we arrived at the mine, Darrell Holbrook, Blackstone, and Sluss had already entered the mine. Darrell's actions that night were heroic. They were cutting through debris, trying to get his crew out, all the while using a methane detector. I remember him lending the detector to someone else and then continuing without it.

"Later, when they found the three survivors, they heard Sutherland calling for help, and that's when they knew they had survivors. Had they not done that, we would have had three more fatalities. Historically, mine rescue teams would never operate without breathing apparatus, but in this case, they did. Had they not taken the risks, there would have been no survivors."

11

The Wait Outside

The next shift, the night shift (known as the "Hoot Owl"), was held outside while the evening shift miners evacuated the mine. By that time, friends, family, neighbors, and other co-workers were also gathering.

The sound of sirens in the night had pierced through their bedtime rituals, warning them of impending tragedy. Everyone knew it was McClure #1 Mine; something had happened at the mine.

Upon arriving, the worst nightmares were confirmed. They were hearing murmurs about the top of the mountain being blown away. They couldn't believe what they were hearing and experiencing.

Each Section of the mine was making their way outside: 1 Left, Caney 1, Caney 4, 3 Left...but where was 2 Left? Over the phone came the call: "2 Left. Pick up. 2 Left. Pick up." It progressed to a frantic cry: "Section 2 Left. Pick up! 2 Left. Pick up!

Anyone from 2 Left, pick up!"

The heart-wrenching plea echoed across the valley, ringing inside the surrounding mountains and into the hearts of the people standing and praying outside.

Shift waiting and family members and friends and neighbors began to gather and start praying for their loved ones. The wait! Unbearable. It wasn't a very long wait. Jarring their souls to the bottom of their stomachs, each one learned of their lost loved ones. As the miners filed out of the mine, they looked around.

No Section 2 Left. Not a one.

12

Preliminary Investigation and Report

Within hours of the explosion, UMWA President Richard L. Trumka arrived at the McClure #1 Mine to join International and District 28 safety experts already on the scene. Trumka took charge of the Union's initial investigation into the causes of the explosion.

Trumka stated, "If the mining laws were obeyed and strictly enforced, something like this could never happen. After his investigation, the Supervisor of the mine promised to take care of things. The Supervisor promised to leave the belt cleanup people on their jobs instead of pulling them off to fill in on the section. He never kept his promises."

In the nine months prior to the June 21 explosion, federal inspectors wrote 167 violations at the McClure #1 Mine. Only 22 were considered "significant and substantial," or worth more than a $20 fine.

Violations considered not to be serious by MSHA included improper ventilation, inadequate rock dust, accumulation of float dust, and accumulation of combustible materials. Mining one entry in each section 22 feet wide in order to place the track and the belt side by side in the same entry. Using belt fly airlocks in place of permanent stoppings between belt and fresh air entries. Cutting 22 feet wide where the battery charging stations are placed in order to store two batteries side by side.

MSHA's past failure to enforce the law shows dramatically when MSHA inspected the mine July 18-20 in preparation for reopening it. This time, feeling the pressure from the UMWA and the spotlight of national publicity, MSHA found 186 violations, including 92 that were considered "significant and substantial," more than four times what it found in the previous nine months.

"It was a pleasure to be turned loose for a change," said one Federal Mine Inspector who took part. "For once, I could do my job the way it's supposed to be done."

Federal records show the mine has been cited for at least 163 health and safety violations since October 1982. Those violations include inadequate ventilation and deficient roof supports.

"Their injury rate is obviously above the national average for coal mines, and there were probably more citations per inspection (than the national average) and more citations at that mine in recent months," said John McGrath, a spokesman for the Federal Mine Safety and Health Administration. "In February 1983, a roof bolter was killed when a portion of the roof caved in."

In fact, McGrath said, a federal inspector had visited the mine on a Tuesday for a spot inspection that is required every five days because the mine emits large amounts of potentially explosive methane. Just two weeks after the McClure disaster, MSHA revoked battery permits at four Clinchfield mines (including McClure #1) where the agency allowed chargers to be placed in passageways for contaminated air.

There had been previous complaints from McClure miners of unsafe conditions, particularly along conveyor belts used to move coal out of the mine. Several bad belt rollers had been found which could generate enough heat to start a fire. It was felt the company had been allowing too much air along belt passageways, a condition that can cause flammable coal dust to accumulate.

Methane levels were reported to be as high as three percent in McClure. MSHA inspector Gerald Sloce, who had been assigned to McClure full-time since October 1982, apparently was the only witness to produce records of methane concentrations greater than one percent.

"Methane can accumulate in a mine very fast," Joseph Corcoran, spokesman for the UMWA, said, "and it can happen with just a minor change in the ventilation system, the mere moving of a single curtain."

Much of Elam's questioning centered around the position of fabric curtains used to control the rate and direction of air flow in Section 2 Left, and he questioned several witnesses extensively on what actions were taken after the opening of a new passageway shortly before the accident.

Union officials insist a ventilation problem must have existed for the explosion to occur. But while the ventilation problem at the 2 Left faces seemed to be solved, mixing the air on the two sections caused a major interruption in ventilation. The UMWA's preliminary report on the disaster states, "This ventilation change, left approximately 3,000 feet of Number 1 and Number 2 Entries of Section Left with no positive means of ventilation in virgin territory along a longwall panel with a history of high methane liberation."

Contained in the entries with "no positive means of ventilation" were the section's power center, the belt, the track, energized trailing cables, and other electrical equipment, all sources of a potentially lethal spark.

Methane had been building up for nearly nine hours. Somewhere there was a spark. At 10:15 p.m., the spark ignited the methane, and the resulting explosion ripped through Section 2 Left, killing seven and injuring three.

13

The Lure of the Mine...

The sky above it glows in the mountain night as if some football stadium was tucked back behind the ridges. And if you wind around the gravel roads far enough, you can just make out its distant roars and groans.

The mine has been called a siren, luring men and women with her song. It is born and bred in the blood of the people living in the Appalachian Mountains. It is what makes coal miners ignore the dangers and warnings and go back underground to work and provide for their families.

Four months after the horrible disaster, McClure #1 Mine was back in operation, pumping coal from the bowels of the westernmost tip of Virginia later to find its way to ships in Hampton Roads.

Miners once again rode a modern elevator that took them 460 feet below the surface to rip coal from rock. But there was an added edge to their efforts since seven of their fellow workers died in a shaft flash fire — the state's worst mine disaster in 25 years.

McClure reopened the day after the disaster occurred for inspectors, and the coal miners volunteered to come back to work. According to the union safety inspector who oversees it, it remains one of Virginia's "hottest" mines — a term used to describe shafts cut into coal deposits that give off large amounts of potentially explosive methane gas.

Survivors of the disaster believe a gas buildup fueled the fatal fire. Because most of the air was apparently blown away momentarily by the June 21 explosion in Section 2 Left at Clinchfield Coal Co.'s McClure #1 Mine, several witnesses said they heard nothing but the popping of their own ears.

The aftershock that came through the passageways of the mine was enough to convince them something had gone terribly wrong.

Miles Sutherland, a roof bolter on Section 2 Left, said he had detected a .9 percent methane reading earlier and had placed a curtain in the area. A later check revealed the level had dropped to a .7 percent.

In underground mines, methane levels of 5-15 percent generally are explosive, but mine-safety officials consider levels higher than 1 percent dangerous. Prescribed amounts of ventilation air are used to rid mines of such gases.

The explosive range of methane is five to 15 percent by volume in air. This means a vapor/air mixture of:
- three percent methane by volume is too rich to burn
- 20 percent methane by volume is too lean to burn
- 10 percent methane by volume is too rich to burn
- five percent methane by volume will give a reading of 100 percent L.E.L. on a combustible gas indicator

Clinchfield officials have said previously that McClure #1, which produces an average of three million cubic feet of methane a day, is their gassiest mine, and one of the gassiest in Virginia.

Monroe West did reveal there have been cases in which methane has ignited at the mine. He said two such ignitions and two fires have been reported. West said both fires occurred at a battery charger located near the bottom of the mine's 460-foot shaft, but he added that neither was reported to federal officials because regulations did not require it.

The coal mine buried here under the tortuous Appalachian Mountains slices through a 40-million-ton seam of high-grade coal. It is the deepest, largest, and best equipped of the mines run by Virginia's largest coal producer at the time.

But ever since it opened in 1979, the miners of this coal-scarred Cumberland Plateau area in far southwest Virginia have been leery of the mine. The 300 miners who did work there spoke often of the mine's overriding menace — methane gas.

McClure #1 is a "hot mine," miners say. Every day it leaks

three million cubic feet of methane into the atmosphere. Some miners feared it could blow at any time.

McClure #1 had received 163 citations for violating health and safety regulations in the past 9 months, including more than 30 for improper or faulty ventilation of methane, federal records show. Its accident rate this year was three times the national average and its fatality rate was nine times above the national norm. A fatality had occurred there every year since 1981. At McClure #1, for all its state-of-the-art equipment, 11 persons have been killed since 1979.

A trade that pays them well, but in return threatens them daily with violent deaths and grinds away at their health. The investigation of the mine explosion started on June 21 and was completed on August 12, 1983, by the Mine Safety & Health Administration (MSHA). They interviewed officials from the State of Virginia, Clinchfield Coal Company, and the United Mine Workers of America, taking sworn statements from 63 people.

According to an article in the *Lebanon News* published on June 29, 1983, a conference was held in Dante with regard to the explosion. Clinchfield President Gene Matthis defended Clinchfield's safety record but did admit McClure #1 was one of the gassiest mines in the state.

14

Co-Workers Remember

Gregory Austin

His Story

Gregory Austin has been enjoying retirement since 2003 with his wife, Diania Howard. They have one daughter, Cindy, and two grandchildren. They have a grandson named Miles, and a granddaughter named Lydia.

"I started working at McClure #1 Mine in September of 1980. After three years as a continuous miner operator helper, the night we all had prayed would never happen, happened. If I remember right, we had already eaten lunch in the dinner hole. My buddy, Johnny Mullins, and I were working as a team. I was helping with the continuous miner, and we were moving between Sections 2 and 3 near the Mains.

"All at once, I was behind the continuous miner, and Johnny was about 20 feet ahead of me on the miner. Then it happened! The sound — it was strange. The miner was right there, but the sound came from 20 or 30 feet ahead of it. I hollered at Johnny, but it was odd. I couldn't hear my voice where I stood; instead, I heard it further ahead. The same thing happened with the sound of the miner. It was like a shock wave, almost like a sonic boom when reentering Earth's atmosphere. We didn't know what had happened.

"At first, I thought there had been a roof fall or something. Things started to get a little dusty, and the dust grew thicker. We became worried. Everyone but the Boss and the Utility Woman headed to the dinner hole. By then, we knew something had gone wrong, and we weren't getting out easily. I said, 'I'll go back and see if I can find them. Don't you all leave here without me.' I went back to the face but didn't see anything. Soon, a Boss and Utility woman were heading our way. They had been in the belt heading between Sections 2 and Section 4.

"We all made our way to the mantrip and began the long journey out. We had to stop several times to clear debris from the track. The track was intact, but it was covered with material blown into it. Timbers had come down everywhere. Some men put on their rescue gear, but I didn't. I was afraid it might get worse, and we'd have to walk out. Those old respirators only lasted about thirty minutes if you were calm and still. Walking or running made them wear out faster. I decided to wait as long as I could. They really don't know how long the rescuers last. We didn't want to find out.

"As we made our way out, I started to smell smoke. It reminded me of a fall evening when a neighbor's coal stove was burning. That scent stuck with me — coal smoke, like the kind I'd smelled as a boy when coal stoves were the only heat we had. We'd filled coal buckets up before dark if it was going to be cold that night to keep us warm.

"Some of the men with rescue masks hadn't pulled the pin to activate them. It was like a hand grenade; if you didn't pull the pin, it didn't work. I'll never forget that. When we got outside, most of the men had made it out, but there was still one section left in Caney Creek. Those miners hadn't known anything had happened. Michael James (that was my buddy), Dave Yates, and I rode to work together. He said, 'We didn't even know anything had happened. They got ahold of us on the phone for them to come out.' They were the last ones to come up.

"The elevator was working to bring miners to the surface, but the wait was long. Tensions were high as everyone wanted out. We were on the other side of Section 2 Left near the Mains, far from where the explosion happened. Still, I believe the air pressure from Section 1 Left to 2 Left caused gas to build up in the Mains and set off the explosion. The gas couldn't dissipate, and something triggered it.

"I think about Cat, who was on the buggy that day, helping with ventilation. I'd signed up for that job but decided against it. Cat got the job instead and was so excited. Women had a harder time working in the mines, and this was an easier job. She used to leave Dr. Pepper cans all through the mine. I think about how God saved me and took her. I still wonder why.

"Emmery Howard returned to work after the explosion and was assigned to me. He was a nervous wreck. One night, we had a 'pop-up,' a small gas bubble that ignites briefly. Emmery thought it was a big explosion and kept stopping the miner to check. The whole experience had messed with his mind. He didn't work much longer after that. Emmery would talk about the men who didn't make it. He said he could hear them praying and calling out. Miles's New Testament was found opened to a scripture about fire and trials. Jimmy and Linda Holbrook even wrote a song about the explosion.

"The explosion happened on June 21 just before our two-week vacation was set to start. Riner, the boss, was retiring that Friday. He'd come down to say goodbye to his men one last time. Little did we know what was about to happen. When we finally made it to the elevator, Joe Huff was there. He said, 'Lord, if you let me out of this crate, I'll never come back.' And he didn't.

"I returned to help clean up. Everything was blackened. Joe had been blown off his feet and his hard hat embedded into his forehead. He survived but suffered short-term memory loss. I never saw him again. Now, Miles was badly burned but kept praying for everyone. I'll never forget seeing him being helped into the ambulance. That image stays with me.

"When the Coal Company offered early retirement in 2003, I took it. After 27 years, I'd had enough. Mining is dangerous work. A federal inspector once told us we had a higher chance of dying in the mine than during two tours in Vietnam. That always stayed with me."

Gregory Austin with co-worker

Lois Bowman

Her Story *(from a prior interview)*

This is Lois Bowman's story, given to the *Coalfield Progress* in 1983.

"The whole crew was in a sweet, kidding mood. I rode down with them in the cage," recalls Lois Bowman of Clintwood, a miner who works a section some distance away.

In another section, about 100 feet from Section 2 Left, nothing seemed out of the ordinary before the explosion. Just before a thick cloud of dust blinded her, she could see the ventilation curtains blown outward. "We had to feel our way out," the miner said.

The men of that section reached their mantrip safely and were on the surface in about 10 minutes, he added. In a different section, about 650 feet above the accident, no sound of explosion could be heard according to another miner who also requested anonymity.

A third miner noted that the remainder of the 84 people in the mine reacted calmly to the disaster. "I was really impressed by how everybody got out," he said. "Nobody panicked. We were out in 15 minutes."

Ms. Bowman, who was working far away from the explosion, didn't hear it either but "knew something was wrong."

At about 10:30 p.m., her section was told to leave the mine but was not told immediately about the explosion.

Many of the miners who reached safety kept a grim, mostly silent vigil outside the mine. The bodies were recovered about 5:30 a.m.

Some of the workers who will be back at work at McClure #1 when the mine reopens are not enthusiastic.

"I have to," said one. "It's the only thing to do around here."

Wade Mullins

His Story

After the explosion and tragic accident at the McClure #1 Mine, those left to mourn the loss of the victims continue to be ever mindful of the occurrence.

As Wade Mullins settled into the rhythm of work inside the McClure #1 Mine, it seemed just like another typical evening shift. But that day, June 21, 1983, would end

Wade Mullins

up being one he and many others in the community will never forget. During that shift, Virginia's worst mining tragedy in 25 years would happen.

This is Wade Mullins' riveting account of that fateful night.

The evening shift had started as a normal, cloudy day. F.C. Riner was talking to the crew, lining them up getting them ready to go to work. He had been training Ernie Hall to take his place because he was ready to retire.

"I hate that so bad for Riner," Mullins said. "He had made it that far, slaving underground, and that happened. It's awful. I went underground at 4:00 p.m. with my buddy and partner, David Stanley. We rode the jeep down to the face of our section, which was called the Main. We traveled a couple of miles to the twin-head Fletcher Roof Bolter machine at the face of the mine which was near Section 2 Left.

"These machines are notoriously loud while you are drilling into the roof. They make a squawking noise. It's so loud you can't even talk to your buddy on the other side. All of a sudden, the lights went off. It was dark. And then they came back on for a few moments, and then the lights went off again."

Mullins suddenly felt a strange sensation and a wave of pressure in his ears. He couldn't hear. The extremely loud roof bolting machine went silent, although he could see it was still running. He wondered if it was him only, or if his partner felt the change, too — although neither man knew what had happened. The section they were working in still had power, so they didn't think anything very bad had happened.

"And we looked at each other and said, 'What in the world was that?' He said, 'We must have had a big roof fall behind us back here somewhere.' I hit my panic bar. We've got a panic bar that we hit with our knee in case something goes wrong to turn the machine off. It stayed off for just a few seconds. It was just a noise, you know, that's how it was to start.

"A second call from the outside came with new instructions. The miners were to take the mantrip as far as they could, monitoring the level of methane gas as they went. At that point, everyone still thought a section of the mine was on fire. The boss came and informed us, 'Leave! Get out! The mine is on fire!' After we heard that, everything was shut down.

"We went to the mantrip getting ready to head outside, and I had my SCR rescuer – all of us did. I had mine between my legs, ready to pop the top off it. So did everybody else. We put them between our legs so we would have them in case we ran into a lot of smoke. When we got down to where you turn up to 2 Left, there was all kinds of smoke coming off that section. Some said the smoke had filled the entire outside holler. We could not go any further on the mantrip jeep. The track was obstructed.

"We had to walk about half a mile from there to the elevator bottom to get out that way. Either that way or walk the slope, and it's all you can do to walk the slope because it's like 1,800 feet down into the bottom, and it was hard to walk up that slope. So, a lot of them rode that three-man cage behind the elevator. They've got a three-man cage back there. Three at a time. The big cage wasn't running to start with, but they got it going. There were 27 people riding it. At first, only the three-man cage was working.

"Miners talked about everybody on that elevator going

down. Some of them might have been on each other's shoulders coming out that night. They talked about everything. Cussing and stuff. Everybody's nose was against the glass looking at the cinder blocks and the concrete coming up out of there. Windows are in the doors where you could see out of the elevator. And cables in the roof, and they would inspect them every now and then to make sure everything was in working order. The inspectors would ride the top of the elevator down, and you could see a little bitty spot way up there where you get off. You could see a little tiny light where you have come down. A light at the end of the tunnel, but it was a light at the end of the cage to the outside.

"We were all talking and wondering what happened, and they said that the blast reached the two air-locked doors, and they said it blowed them wide open. That's why the air quality was so poor. There was good air until you got to where 2 Left came out where Sutherland worked. There was a lot of smoke we ran into there. And we had to walk, like I said, because a jeep was turned sideways on the rails. We were all scared to death for our lives.

"So, the mine phone kept saying, '2 Left! 2 Left! 2 Left! Anybody on 2 Left, give me a holler! Holler! Anybody on 2 Left?' We've got that speaker on the phone that goes over the mine over the Section. Nobody ever would answer it, so they knew it was 2 Left. They kept on hollering and hollering until someone picks that phone up. Nobody picked it up. That answer never came. Dead Silence.

"The men walked from there, a distance of 1,000 feet or more, to a service elevator that would take three men at a time to the surface. Although they weren't certain, the smoke and dust coming from Section 2 Left indicated it was the section on fire."

The miners were able to ride the smaller elevator, which had power from a separate source, to the surface. It would be nearly an hour later, once Mullins and the other miners working in his section reached the outside, that he knew the mine had exploded.

"When we opened the elevator door, rescue people were there. It was then we learned there had been an explosion."

Mullins and the crew of men he worked with had no communication with the outside from the time they left their section until they reached the outside.

"The first person they brought out was Miles Sutherland. He was in bad shape. His snowy white hair was burned and melted to the scalp. He was black all over. Hollering. Praying. 'Oh, Lord. Oh, Lord.' I saw that, and I thought, 'It was an actual explosion.' He kept repeating, 'Oh, Lord. Oh, Lord.' And that was just, 'Shew. Lord, have mercy.' I could see him crying and he made it to the top of the elevator, so he was thanking the Lord for it when they got off. That means a lot.

"I decided when I saw Sutherland, I was heading home. Me and Kemper Damer showered together. The showers outside and everything were working all right, so it didn't kick the outside power."

Seeing his friend injured so badly made the explosion real to Mullins. He knew then there was little hope for any of the miners working in that section.

"The rescue team told us that Emmery Howard was still alive, and Joe Boyd was still alive, and Miles. That's the only ones. The other ones got killed. Both of the bosses got killed."

After every shift, Mullins would always call Angie, his fiancé, but someone else called her that night to tell her of the explosion. "They asked if I was her fiancé, then told her, 'I just heard McClure #1 Mine blowed the whole top of the mountain off.'"

Angie panicked and woke her parents, but her dad believed it was just a prank call. She wasn't satisfied, however, until her mom drove her to the mine. There she ran into a man who worked with Mullins. He assured her that Mullins was safe and was on his way home.

It was a day or two after the explosion that Mullins realized what a close call he'd had, because McClure #1 was a union mine; job openings there were posted. He had signed for the shuttle car operator position held by Mary Kathleen Counts, the woman killed in the explosion. He said Counts had previously shoveled the belt line, a cold and unpleasant job. Mullins felt sorry for her working in the cold, though, so he erased his name from the job posting when he saw that she, too, had signed up for it. If Mullins hadn't erased his name from the job posting, he may have been killed in the explosion.

So many stories of survival; stories of families who lost a loved one. Switching of jobs. Retiring that week. Three days left until vacation. A foreman who was not supposed to be underground the last week of his duties. One had a toothache but went to work anyway.

Mullins thinks back to the brothers and friends and co-workers that were killed that fateful night and remembers the way they all laughed and joked each day before going underground. Some playing horseshoe. Some just catching up on the job that needed to be done.

He recalled that Cat Counts would drink Dr. Pepper every day. "When she emptied each pop can, she would hang it on a wire or a roof bolt place," Mullins said. "You would see the pop cans hanging near the belt line and know where Cat ate lunch. When I would see the pop cans, it would make me smile and think about Cat.

"I went back in there when they started recovering and rebuilding everything. We had a crew go in there, but you had two federal mine inspectors with every crew that went with us to keep monitoring gas. We had to rebuild several ventilation brattices from the mouth of Section 2 Left all the way to the face of the mine where all the miners were working. A brattice is a partition or a shaft lining in a coal mine, typically made of wood or heavy cloth, that is used to control ventilation in a mine. Brattices are built between columns in a mine to direct airflow."

McClure was described as a major explosion, having more power behind it than the Scotia mine disaster in Oven Fork, Kentucky, in 1976. A total of 26 miners were killed in separate explosions within a two-day period. It blew equipment and parts half a mile away.

"When I went back to work, I was kind of nervous that I didn't want that to happen again, but it should be under control. I hoped. I am trained in methane detection. My dad was a Fire Boss. Sutherland had a rescuer with him because he was a roof bolter. All roof bolters have to have a methane detection system and pass the tests to get your card. I had federal and state.

"McClure Mine was probably about two or three miles from the elevator to the Main. McClure traveled all the way to Route 83 past Freemont heading toward Clintwood. It had a shop underground that was as big as Irwin Supply. All the parts, pieces, belts, and everything. It was huge. We got our supplies off the railcars and took them back there and stocked them.

"I think there were four big, long aisles with parts bins and stuff that you could go there and get whatever you needed. It was set up with a telephone and everything. We were underneath the earth. I always thought about whenever I worked there that I'm right below the river that I got baptized in. Mc-

Clure River right there at Freemont is where we had a baptizing place right across from the Highway Department. That's what I always thought. If this water breaks in on us, it's the same water that I got baptized in.

"I worked at Roaring Fork up past Ervinton High School for Alpha Resources the last time I worked in the mines, until I ended up with black lung, seriously affecting my health and way of life. Miles went through a lot while he was over there. He worked at Camp Branch with Daddy. I miss Miles so bad. Every one of them. It hurts me so bad that F.C. only had three more days until retirement. He was there training Ernie Hall, and they both got killed. I hate to say that, but I know both of them. F.C. was a very good boss and good man.

"I got to take my wife, Angie, underground there. We rode in there and she said, 'Why, you've got it made. It's pitch black and you can't see nothing.'"

When Mullins took a job at Clinchfield's McClure #1 Mine a year before the explosion, he knew its reputation for being gaseous. His dad, Billy Gene Mullins, had worked day shift there since the mine opened. Like other miners, he ignored the inherent danger of any coal mining job and accepted the position. Mining was in his blood, after all. He wanted to follow in the footsteps of his father and was willing to accept the risks that went along with the job.

Wade and his fiancée, Angie Rasnick, got married in 1982, making their current home in Bluff City, Tennessee. They have two grown children, Christopher and Julia Leann, and four grandchildren, Christopher Caleb, Mason Ryan, Layla Leann, and Leslie Brook.

"I was probably 25 when the explosion happened. I'm 66 now and struggling with black lung."

Mullins vividly recalls that sad night and recalls the details of it. He also still thinks of and dearly misses the seven miners lost to the explosion. "God was there in the fire that night with the three survivors. He was the fourth man. I think about it a lot during the time of the year when it happened. Each and every one of them there was just as close as family. Everyone was like family. It is a brotherhood. We have a bond.

"I knew all of them well. I worked with them every day. I miss them, and every time something comes on the news about a cave-in or explosion, I think back. These men will never be forgotten."

Ronnie Mann

His Story

"I started working for Clinchfield in July 1974 at the Birchfield Mine in Wise County, Virginia, and in July 1981, I started at the McClure #1 Mine in McClure, Virginia.

"I was first a utility man on the First Left Section on the second shift and was awarded a shuttle car operator's position on the same shift. In June 1983, the company posted a locomotive operator position on the day shift, and I signed up to see if I could get that job. As it happened, I was the senior person to apply for that position and it was awarded to me.

"A few days later on June 21, I was dispatched to the First Left Section to transport supplies to that section. We arrived on the section about 3:00 p.m., dropped the flat car loaded with supplies, and headed back to the area where we would leave the locomotives for the next shift. By this time, our shift was ending, and we proceeded to go to the elevator and leave the mine for home.

"I arrived home about 5:30 p.m., ate supper with my family, and about 10:30 p.m. as I was getting ready for bed, I received a phone call from my good friend, Roy Glovier, who was a mechanic on the evening shift, and he told me there had been an accident at the mine, but he wasn't sure what happened. He said, 'The mine is being evacuated.'

"Roy said, 'It appears that everyone is out of the mine except my previous section.' I said, 'Oh, no. My friends are there.' Cat Counts had taken my previous position on the shuttle car, and my good friend, Miles Sutherland, and Eugene Meade shared a ride with me. All the other guys that I worked with were there. As the night passed by, I sat by the phone and waited to hear what had happened. Roy called again and said, 'There was a fire and probably a methane explosion.' I found out the next day that it was indeed an explosion and there were fatalities.

"Cat Counts perished and six other crew members. I learned that Miles was alive but barely hanging on and probably would not make it. As I wiped away my tears, I began to realize I would have been there if I hadn't gone to day shift. For my family's sake, I felt good about that, but down deep inside I felt really bad that Cat had taken my place. Heaven spared me for a reason, and so I thanked my God for His mercy.

"The mine was shut down for repairs for a few weeks, and I was selected to help with repairs and rebuilding. Miles was sent to the Burn Center, and when he was allowed to go home from the hospital, I went to visit him. We hugged and I told him I was so happy that he was still with us. He had spent many months in the hospital, and it was so hard what he had to endure. There were many prayer warriors calling out his name to the mighty Lord.

"Miles shared with me what he remembered, and I knew it was very difficult for him to talk about it. He said, 'After the fire ripped through, I was knocked unconscious. I remember waking up and in total darkness, and I was really trying to breathe. My hands were burned so bad that I could not open my self-rescuer. I laid back down on the floor and told the Lord I surrender my spirit into your hands.' He continued, 'I recall waking up and I was on a hospital bed, and I was being moved. I realized I was being transported to a hospital.' He passed out again, and the next time he became conscious, he was at the hospital.

"My two brothers, Danny and Ricky, were part of the rescue team that went in to get the workers out, and they said that Miles actually opened his eyes on the mine elevator as they were transporting Miles to the surface.

"Sometime later, a few years, I spoke with Miles, and he was doing pretty good. He was looking good, considering what he had been through. His faith in Jesus had only gotten stronger, and what an inspiration he was to me and those around him. I said, 'Brother, would you be up to sharing your testimony with my church sometime?' And he flatly said, 'No, I am not ready to do that. This is my encounter and true.'"

15

Conclusion

FACTS:

At approximately 10:15 p.m. on June 21, 1983, an explosion occurred on Section 2 Left of the McClure #1 Mine of Clinchfield Coal Company located at McClure, Dickenson County, Virginia. Seven coal miners were killed. Three other miners were injured but survived the explosion.

INVESTIGATION RESULTS:

The explosion occurred as the result of a failure to install proper ventilation apparatus at Crosscut #40 when Section 2 Left cut into the setup entries of Section 1 Left. The failure to properly separate the two air currents caused a significant ventilation change in Section 2 Left.

The air coming across the setup entries continued through the working face of Section 2 Left and out the return. This restricted the ventilating current of number 2 and number 3 Entries of Section 2 Left.

The ventilating current in number 2 and number 3 Entries of Section 2 Left was restricted to a point that an adequate velocity of air did not exist to dilute and carry away the methane being liberated. The lack of adequate air velocity allowed methane to accumulate to an explosive level.

EXTENT OF FORCES:

It was apparent that the accident was primarily a methane explosion with primary cause being methane. Evidence of force was observed at the power center where a lid was blown off. The battery covers were blown off the scoop, and the welder was blown over on its side. A few timbers were down along the beltline. The high voltage splice box at number 27 Crosscut was damaged and blown in an outby direction for approximately 140 feet. Stoppings were blown out or blown over throughout the section. The stoppings were constructed of concrete blocks, stacked dry, and plastered. Not all stoppings were blown down, but very little force is required to dislodge stoppings constructed in this manner.

EXTENT OF FLAME:

Although coal dust did not enter significantly into the explosion, coal dust in the entries did contribute to the total length of explosion flame. Evidence of flame was found to extend approximately 2,400 feet in the number two Entry of Section 2 Left, approximately 2,600 feet in number three

Entry, and approximately 2,600 feet in number four Entry. Evidence of flame stopped at Crosscut 15 and number two Entry and stopped at Crosscut 13 in number three Entry.

Evidence of flame extended across the setup entries to their intersection with Section 1 Left. This evidence was in the form of coke, soot, melted plastic brattice material, charred paper, charred cable insulation, and other burned material.

Some of the victims received severe burns while some appeared to have no burns. Some of the victims' clothing exhibited signs of flame.

MSHA INVESTIGATION:

MSHA investigators concluded that the primary cause of the explosion was the failure of mine management to maintain sufficient volume and velocity of air in the number two and number three Entries of Section 2 Left to dilute, render harmless, and carry away the methane gas being liberated in those Entries.

About nine hours before the explosion, the #40 Crosscut of Section 2 Left was cut through into the longwall setup entries. A failure to install ventilation controls to separate the air split, ventilating the longwall setup entries from the air split ventilating the Section 2 Left Entries, affected the movement of air.

The explosive atmosphere was ignited by electrical arcing created by one of six possible sources:

1. Interruption of the belt control circuit
2. A ground fault in the trailing cable for the conveyor belt feeder
3. Interruption of the dinner hole light circuit
4. Normal operation of the non-permissible personnel carrier
5. Automatic operation of one of the circuit breakers in the Section power center
6. A fault in the cable plug for the continuous mining machine trailing cable

16

Aftermath

As of publication date, McClure #1 Mine has changed entrance portals and is now working across from the closed opening as McClure #41.

The investigation started on June 21 and was completed on August 12, 1983, by the Mine Safety & Health Administration (MSHA). They interviewed officials from the State of Virginia, Clinchfield Coal Company, and the United Mine Workers of America, taking sworn statements from 63 people.

The coalfields of the Appalachian Mountains in its day provided a very comfortable living for this region in providing heat and electricity.

You have to have coal to provide solar panels to work, and windmills. When there is no sun, you have no heat. When there is no wind, you have no power. God is providing us a new morning. He provided us with the resource to provide our essential needs.

It's been over four decades since the McClure #1 Mine

accident. The shockwaves have rippled over the years, and today it's still remembered. Because of the disaster, increased regulations came about that helped improve safety for all miners. It is hoped that this book will honor our miners and help people remember that they provided an energy source that is in high demand throughout the world. The things we take for granted, they give their life for. Blood, sweat, and sunless days buy our electricity. Without them, we'd be in the dark.

Epilogue

Marsha Sutherland Self

In writing this book, Becky and I have been on the most wonderful adventure of a lifetime. God has led the way and has opened so many doors to so many people, that our faith has been strengthened. It has been a task that has lasted for two and a half years.

So many thanks go out to all of the coal miners and their families, and the families of the survivors of that fateful night that should never be forgotten.

Our journey has been tiring, exhausting, overwhelming, sad, tearful yet joyful, inspiring, loving, full of friendship, caring, providing, laughing, and above all of this, prayer before we begin each day.

1 Corinthians 10:31 has been a mantra for us:
"Whatever you do, do all to the Glory of God."
AMEN.

I Wish I Had Touched Your Face

The last day I saw you,
I wish I had touched your face.
You were standing in the sun,
Mid-day had begun...
I will forever see you
Standing in that place.

Saying our goodbyes always made me blue,
And I already missed you as we embraced.
I only wish I knew what was about to come true.
I wish when we hugged, I had touched your face.

I wish I held you longer, wish my hug was stronger,
Wish I gave you much more grace.
While giving you that final kiss goodbye,
I wish I had touched your face.

If I had known you were passing on,
Going to a better place,
I would have taken the time to hold you longer...
I wish I had touched your face.

– Rebecca Riner White

About the Authors

MARSHA SELF is a coal miner's daughter from Dickenson County. She graduated from Castlewood and SWVA Community College. She worked at UMWA District 28 Office, followed by the UMWA and Bituminous Coal Wage Agreement in Washington. Upon returning to Abingdon, she married Randall Self and began Appalachian Court Reporting in 1991. Becoming an author inspired her to open another business — For C's: Christ, Country, Coal, Children.

REBECCA RINER WHITE is also a coal miner's daughter, from Dickenson County, Virginia. She is a graduate of Castlewood High School, Hiwassee College, and the University of Tennessee. Becky worked in Learning Resources in Knox County, Tennessee, and Washington County, Virginia. She and her husband, Samuel, make their home in Bristol, Virginia. Becky enjoys Bible study, reading, writing, and poetry.

Thank You

The authors want to thank all the readers of this adventure that we have taken about mining and especially sharing the working lives of our dads. We also want to take the time to thank all of you who helped us share this bittersweet true story that affected so many lives. There have been so many new people that we have met, and they have shared their stories and opened their hearts to us. God bless all of you.

Miles Sutherland's mining hat and New Testament

Resources

Clinch Valley Times

Coalfield Progress Newspaper, special noted Jenay Tate for her expert contributions.

Dickenson Star

Memories from Dante, Katherine C. Shearer, November 2001

Mine Safety & Health Administration

Roanoke Times

Teresa Hawkins Mullins and Jim Scott Mullins, authors of *Holly Creek*

The Bristol Herald Courier

The Virginia Pilot

The Washington Post

U.M.W.A. Mining Journal

www.ingramcontent.com/pod-product-compliance
Lightning Source LLC
Chambersburg PA
CBHW022009160426
43197CB00007B/347